EDITED BY ETHAN HAIMO AND PAUL JOHNSON

Stravinsky Retrospectives

UNIVERSITY OF NEBRASKA PRESS   LINCOLN AND LONDON

Copyright 1987 by the
University of Nebraska Press
All rights reserved
Manufactured in the United
States of America

The paper in this book meets
the minimum requirements
of American National
Standard for Information
Sciences–Permanence
of Paper for Printed Library
Materials, ANSI Z39.48-1984.

Library of Congress
Cataloging–in–Publication Data
Main entry under title:
Stravinsky retrospectives.
Includes index.
Contents: Stravinsky's
"fortunate continuities"
and "legitimate accidents,"
1882–1982 / William Austin –
Stravinsky's verticals and
Schoenberg's diagonals:
a twist of fate / Milton
Babbitt – Problems of hierarchy
in Stravinsky's Octet /
Ethan Haimo – [etc.]
1. Stravinsky, Igor,
1882–1971 – Criticism and
interpretation–Addresses,
essays, lectures.
I. Haimo, Ethan, 1950–
II. Johnson, Paul, 1954–
ML410.S932S794   1987
780'.92'4   86–1262
ISBN 0–8032–2335–8
(alkaline paper)

Contents

Preface

Thirteen years after his death Stravinsky remains as important and fascinating a figure as he was during his life. Both his music and personality still command a level of attention, interest, and respect afforded very few figures in music history.

Of course, the nature of our relationship with him and his music has changed. No longer do we wait with excitement and curiosity to see what new direction his ever fertile imagination would take him. Nor can we wonder what unexpectedly different compositions might appear, challenging afresh our notion of the Stravinsky "style." No more do we expect to be given a new and piquantly different glass through which to examine yet another corner of our musical past. Nor can we anticipate still more perceptive, outrageous, trenchant, cultured, witty, and thought-provoking comments on music, musicians, and society. All that is past.

With the hindsight of thirteen years, it is now beginning to be possible to gain a perspective on Stravinsky's achievement as a whole—to see more clearly his effect on his contemporaries and to begin to make some estimation of his position in history. As we look back at him, at his life, his career and works, we become keenly aware that the very process of looking back keeps him part of our current musical lives: not just part of our past but of our present and future as well. Like all great composers of the past, he continually exerts his influence on our consciousness each time we think about him, discuss his contributions, hear his music, analyze his scores, or argue about the aesthetic he represented. We should not forget that many of the compositional problems Stravinsky faced are still central to contemporary compositional thinking. Questions of hierarchy, the function of rhythm in non-tonal music, the nature of form, notions of interval, and above all, the ephemeral search for compositional direction are all problems the contemporary composer faces daily and were all faced squarely, and inimitably, by Stravinsky. The musical solutions he advanced have the potential to influence another generation of musicians, but only if his contributions are examined and understood.

In some ways we are fortunate in Stravinsky research. So much is known about him and so much material is available. We are presented with a figure whose biography (except for his childhood) is extraordinarily well documented. We know where he was, what he did, and when he did it. We know the people with whom he collaborated. We have a wealth of primary source material: manuscripts, sketchbooks, conversations, letters, recordings, an autobiography, and much more. Such a wealth and degree of information is virtually unprecedented in music history. It effectively frees us to concentrate on a wide range of substantive musical issues.

Certainly there is no shortage of important issues that need to be addressed, for although an enormous amount of attention has been given to Stravinsky, much of that has been biographical, and relatively little has taken the form of detailed examination of his music. Indeed, compared to our understanding of tonal music, it is clear that we have only begun to understand the structural underpinnings of even one of his several styles. Much serious thinking has to be done about his pitch organization, the large-scale formal design, the nature of harmonic progression, the meaning and function of referential sonorities, and how all interact with Stravinksy's intricate rhythms. We need to develop a convincing stylistic portrait of his music—not only to differentiate between the various periods but to identify the features common to all. The published writings and the treasure trove of unpublished, largely unexamined papers, sketches, and workbooks present fertile ground for study. Attempts have to be made to reconcile the contradictions and clarify the cryptic statements scattered through his writings. A critical, even skeptical approach must be taken in attempting to correlate his writings with his music, always remembering how conscious Stravinsky was of his public image and recognizing how such consciousness can shape and direct the content of such comments.

It was for an understanding of these kinds of questions that an in-depth study of Stravinsky's music seemed a particularly worthwhile venture. Now, more than a century after his birth, it seems reasonable to expect that a serious examination of his works could yield important results and that persuasive answers might be found to some of the perplexing problems posed by his music. It was this belief that motivated the editors to plan this volume, the questions described above serving as an outline that guided us as we sought out appropriate contributors. We had in mind a balance, even synthesis, between theory and musicology, between established scholars and younger contributors. We wanted consideration of Stravinsky's early, middle, and late works, and analyses both of individual works and broader stylistic trends. The result is this volume, and we hope that the questions it raises and the issues it illuminates will help keep Stravinsky's music in the forefront of our musical consciousness.

William Austin's paper, and the questions it raises, provide a keynote to our collection, and it is a fortunate accident that the alphabet places it first. His investigation, inspired by passages in Stravinsky's *Poetics,* leads him to consider Stravinsky's position in history from Stravinsky's own aesthetic perspective. This is a fascinating idea, multilayered, which leads to a multitude of further questions about the relationship of a composer to history, to his forerunners and followers, but also sheds light on Stravinsky's own view of himself circa 1940. The intricacy of the many questions in this paper are their own reward, for they provide a framework into which the other essays of this book can be placed and a perspective on the responses those authors offer to some of the challenging questions posed by Stravinsky's life and work.

Milton Babbitt's article addresses a repertoire that epitomized the unpredictability of Stravinsky's stylistic path. At the time, certainly, Stravinsky's turn to the twelve-tone system surprised his critics and stunned his followers. Yet notwithstanding the attention that this apparent stylistic revolution has drawn, the inner workings of his technique have remained unclear: Stravinsky's use of the twelve-tone system is no mere copy of Schoenberg's, far from it. His is a unique adaptation with its own operations and transformations of the referential material. In his article Babbitt not only clarifies the meaning of Stravinsky's verticals and diagonals but also, as in so many of his articles on the twelve-tone system, goes far beyond the local analytical issues to an exposition and discussion of the systematic implications of the material. Babbitt has thus provided the tools with which to analyze some of Stravinsky's twelve-tone works and at the same time has opened up a new area for theoretical and compositional exploration.

Stravinsky's "centric" music presents a different set of theoretical challenges. As in his twelve-tone works, Stravinsky clearly offers a new way of organizing and relating pitches. However, there are also unmistakable similarities with common-practice tonality. Theorists have been torn between the need to create autonomous theoretical formulations that might account for this music in a persuasive way and the understandable tendency to employ concepts and terms derived from tonal music. Ethan Haimo, Paul Johnson, and Joseph Straus examine the problems this music presents in three different ways.

Haimo begins by examining the concept of hierarchy from the level of detail on up to the large-scale formal structure in an analysis of the first movement of the Octet. By adapting concepts from tonal theory, but defining them in new ways, he offers a view of the hierarchical relationships in this composition that is self-contained, yet takes into account the kinship with tonal music.

Straus also analyzes the Octet (and two other works) in his study of sonata form in Stravinsky. In spite of Stravinsky's label as a neoclassic composer, his works include a relatively small number of movements that resemble the classic thematic pattern. Stravinsky's use of such formal patterns raises an important issue: What is the relationship between the form of these works and the tonal procedures that underlie them? Although this is the problem that is addressed in the paper, its further implications relate again to a central problem of pitch hierarchy in twentieth-century music: What is (or even, what should be) the relationship between the local pitch organization and the large-scale formal plan of a composition not organized in terms of standard practice tonality?

Stravinsky's centric music has been divided into two distinct periods: Russian and neoclassic. Such stylistic categories highlight the differences that divide Stravinsky's work, deflecting our attention from those characteristics that cut across such stylistic boundaries. In his essay, Paul Johnson suggests a way to view these two periods as embracing important shared compositional techniques. The tools used for analyzing these techniques are derived from the theory of atonal music, employing its sophisticated ways of describing the intervallic properties of collections. Perhaps the internal similarities seen here can help show that the dichotomies between the Russian and neoclassic works are not so much contradictions as different interpretations of similar constructive ideas.

The relationship of Stravinsky's neoclassic works to composers of the past (Machaut, Bach, Gesualdo, Beethoven, and others) has been analyzed in great detail. Yet surprisingly little has been said about his music's relationship to his immediate past—to the music of his Russian predecessors and to the folk and popular traditions current in the Russia of his youth. In the West, particularly, this may be due to an unfamiliarity both with the Russian language and the musical repertoire of late nineteenth-century Russia. But whatever the reasons, there are significant blank spots in our knowledge of Stravinsky's Russian character and background and the influence they had on all aspects of his music.

For example: How much and what kind of influence on Stravinsky's works can be ascribed to those Russian composers whose works dominated the stage and concert hall of Stravinsky's youth? The answer to this question can come only through an informed comparison, based on intimate knowledge, both of Stravinsky's works and those of his Russian predecessors. Yet with the exception of some well-known instances, such influence is not to be identified in terms of consciously explicit quotes or imitations. The challenge then is to establish a set of criteria whereby such suspected influences can be isolated and identified. In a study of this sort, no individual example could be conclusive in isolation. Rather, the range of examples introduced by Claudio Spies creates the framework for a proper understanding of the degree and type of influence exerted on Stravinsky by Rimsky, Tchaikovsky, and others. The comparison of dozens of works creates, in the most effective manner, the proper context for judging how Stravinsky "borrowed" from his predecessors.

A specific kind of Russian influence is seen in Stravinsky's text setting, as Richard Taruskin demonstrates. One of the criticisms leveled against Stravinsky's vocal music is that his text setting is crude, violating the natural rhythms of the text. It has also been asserted that this is particularly so in those of his compositions that use non-Russian texts, the implication being that there might be a more orthodox treatment in those works where the language was Stravinsky's native tongue than in those whose texts were in the languages that Stravinsky learned with varying degrees of fluency after leaving Russia. Taruskin effectively demolishes these criticisms, showing that it was not difficulties of language that determined the character of his text settings but rather conscious compositional decisions. By looking chronologically at Stravinsky's Russian text settings, Taruskin shows that the alleged crudities were deliberate, and that understanding their compositional purpose is crucial to understanding the stylistic development of Stravinsky's rhythm.

Whether or not Stravinsky will eventually be viewed as a "fiery beacon" or will be consigned to the "margins of history" is beyond our ability to foretell. What we can hope is that through this collection we will contribute to a better understanding and appreciation of his music, and through that process keep our relationship to the past as constructive and vivid as was Stravinsky's. It is to that end that we present these studies.

ACKNOWLEDGMENTS

The seven papers of this volume were originally presented at the Stravinsky Centennial Conference at the University of Notre Dame, November 22–23, 1982. In addition to the seven lectures, two concerts and a panel discussion were presented. The Alice Tully Foundation is to be thanked for its generous financial assistance, as is the Institute for Scholarship in the Liberal Arts of the University of Notre Dame. In addition, the editors would like to thank Calvin Bower, chairman of the Department of Music at the University of Notre Dame for his support of this enterprise. Carl Stam, conductor of the Notre Dame Chorale, presented a fine concert of Stravinsky's choral works at the conference. Celia Felix typed and proofread the entire manuscript. Claudio Spies was very helpful in suggestions for organization and topics to be discussed.

The following kindly granted permission for the reproduction of music examples: Paul Sacher Foundation; European American Music; Boosey and Hawkes; J & W Chester/Edition Wilhelm Hansen London, Ltd.; Dover Publications; C. F. Peters Corporation; and Kalmus.

ETHAN HAIMO

PAUL JOHNSON

Stravinsky's "FORTUNATE CONTINUITIES"

AND "LEGITIMATE ACCIDENTS," 1882–1982

WILLIAM AUSTIN | *Cornell University*

1. *Poetique musicale,* the Charles Eliot Norton Lectures delivered in 1939–40, published in French 1942; the translation by Ingolf Dahl and Arthur Knodel appeared separately in 1947 as *Poetics of Music in the Form of Six Lessons;* with a preface by Darius Milhaud this translation was reprinted in 1956 and thereafter (New York: Vintage Press). The bilingual edition, with French and English on facing pages, had a new preface, by George Seferis; it appeared in 1970 (Cambridge: Harvard University Press). Page 92 in the 1970 edition is the source of the quotation here. Further references to follow will be identified by page numbers for the same edition (in parentheses in the text).

Are continuities and accidents opposites?

The adjectives that Stravinsky applies to them suggest an intimate relationship, maybe like yin and yang: "fortunate continuities" and "legitimate accidents." In his *Poetics of Music*[1] he goes a little beyond mere suggestion. He stimulates me to try exploring his idea, to apply it tentatively to his own life and works, and to their reception and interpretation so far, sometimes to turn it against one or another of his polemical thoughts, in order to clear a path for other people in accordance with their own varying knowledge and interests. First, let me summarize Stravinsky's own context for the terms I have picked out.

In parentheses I must acknowledge that the *Poetics* owes much of its wording and some of its ideas to Roland-Manuel, Pierre Suvchinsky, Paul Valéry, and even Jean Cocteau, along with other thinkers whose contributions have not yet been traced. It would be wonderful to discover Roland-Manuel's notes or drafts. Short of that, it *will* be wonderful some day to study the books and clippings in Stravinsky's archive, with their marginalia, which not even Robert Craft has yet surveyed. Eventually there will be a better context than anyone can have today for understanding Stravinsky's mind. But now it is permissible, I think, to call the text of the *Poetics* Stravinsky's own context for the terms "continuities" and "accidents."

In the fourth lesson of the six that compose the *Poetics,* Stravinsky announces his wish to "establish a picture in perspective, a stereoscopic view of the history of my art" (p. 88). He proposes to contribute something toward the "examination of the problem of style" (p. 90). He begins with Mozart and Haydn, whose similarities and differences are both familiar to his listeners, he presumes.

I

There is no need to tell you that what is called the style of an epoch results from a combination of individual styles, a combination which is dominated by the methods of the composers who have exerted a preponderant influence on their time . . . Mozart and Haydn . . . benefited from the same culture, drew on the same sources, and borrowed each other's discoveries. Each of them, however, works a miracle all his own. . . . The masters, who in all their greatness surpass the generality of their contemporaries, send out the rays of their genius well beyond their own day. In this way they appear as powerful signal-fires—as beacons which shine out . . . upon the historical field of art and promote that continuity which gives the true and only legitimate meaning to a word much abused . . . evolution. [p. 92]

This "fortunate continuity [*heureuse continuité*]," he goes on, "makes possible the development of culture." It resembles

a general rule that suffers few exceptions, which, one might say, were expressly made to confirm it. One sees as if silhouetted on the far horizon of art, from time to time, one of those erratic blocks whose origin is unknown and whose existence is incomprehensible. These monoliths seem heaven-sent to affirm the existence, and in a certain measure the legitimacy, of the accidental [*légitimité de l'accidental*]. These elements of discontinuity, these freaks of nature, bear various names in our art. The most curious is named Hector Berlioz. [p. 92]

These excerpts from the *Poetics* may be familiar. The metaphor of beacon-fires, borrowed from Baudelaire, is fresh, apt, and memorable. The estimate of Berlioz is not so fresh, but hard to forget. The relation between continuities and accidents is not emphasized enough to prevail over such details. But this relation is my topic. Let me continue trying to clarify the relation, in the hazy "perspective view" that the *Poetics* provides.

When Stravinsky views the twentieth century, or perhaps especially the 1930s, he deplores a "musical culture that is day by day losing the sense of continuity. . . . Individual freak and intellectual anarchy . . . tend to control the world. . . . The erratic block is no longer an exceptional curiosity; it is the only model offered to neophytes for emulation . . ." (p. 94). Stravinsky's immediate predicament is the foundation of his view of the nineteenth century. He has confessed as much, in his introductory lecture (p. 34) and again in the third (p. 62). His dogmatism is not merely a personal apology, but it is based on his practical experience and this is part of the dogma. As you may recall, he goes on in the fourth lecture to wrestle with the terms "modernism" and "academicism" and finally to rail against "snobisme" and "pompierisme." This railing may have seemed to him in later decades somewhat quaint, or at least inadequate. To listeners like me in 1939 it was more welcome and more memorable than the ideas of continuity and accident. The fourth lecture ends without establishing a clear "picture in perspective" or ever examining the "problem of style" in any systematic way. But the idea of continuities is to return soon.

The fifth lecture, on Russian music, traces continuities from Glinka through Rimsky and Tchaikovsky. Never claiming for these composers that they were "great beacon-fires," Stravinsky affirms that, "whatever one may think of these tendencies, they were comprehensible and legitimate. . . . They took their place within the framework of Russian history" (p. 126). He presupposes a framework. He places tendencies and individual composers within it. Then he proceeds to his painful confrontation with Soviet policies, where the framework narrows and excludes him. By 1962, when he visited the USSR, he recognized his pages on this topic as too simple, though in the epilogue to the *Poetics* he had referred to the fifth lecture as offering an example of the "biography of music" that he proposed in the fourth.

The last lecture, concerned chiefly with performance, does not explicitly return to the relation between continuities and accidents. By implication, both are subordinate to the polemical dogmas of dynamic order, equilibrium, and unity.

My effort to explore further the idea of continuities and accidents detaches it from the polemical dogmas. I shall return, at the end of this essay, to the first half of the *Poetics* and especially the second lesson, with its account of the composer's "appetite" and "inspiration." But now I turn away from the immediate context to use the idea independently, applying it first to views of history broader than those Stravinsky set forth in 1939–40. Then I shall apply it to his own work.

A "fortunate continuity" cannot be guaranteed or taken for granted. It is a "true evolution," distinct from such other continuities as mere routines of craft and routine academic theories. Moreover, the "rule" of true continuity is surprisingly "confirmed" by "legitimate accidents," which are distinct from rebellions or alleged revolutions. The composers whose radiance "promotes" a favorite continuity, Haydn and Mozart, may be "heaven-sent" accidents. To call them accidents may be just as appropriate as to call Berlioz a "freak." Stravinsky points out that the "beacon-fires" cause disturbance. History continues, but not "without shock nor without accident." Stravinsky never personifies his "continuity." Rather he defines it by referring to individuals and their concrete interactions. So he might at least acknowledge the possibility that a "freak" like Berlioz could eventually prove to be a "beacon-fire," promoting continuity, despite the discontinuity of his work with his near-contemporaries. Might Stravinsky tolerate the idea of a continuity from Berlioz to Edgard Varèse and Pierre Boulez? from Berlioz to Olivier Messiaen and Boulez? He did come to admire Varèse and Boulez and to acknowledge the prevailing influence of Messiaen. I think he would have liked my notion of their "legitimizing" Berlioz. In any case, this notion can help to take hold of his complementary, dialectical concepts.

Continuities are sought and criticized by musicologists. Many scholars are concerned to clarify and strengthen a continuity from Bach and earlier composers to present concerns. Stravinsky did not cite Bach in his 1939 sketch of "a picture in perspective." He was only beginning to make acquaintance with Willi Apel and Archibald Davison, whose *Harvard Anthology of Music* was in preparation; this anthology, as Richard Taruskin has observed, was to furnish Stravinsky with many later references.[2] I suggest that he would have welcomed the development of his idea to include the fortunate continuity from Josquin, Palestrina, and Bach. He might have recognized the contributions to that continuity by the pioneer musicologist Johann Forkel and his noble patron Gottfried van Swieten, as well as the later contributions, more widely acknowledged, by a fortunate continuer like Mendelssohn and more dogged continuers like Brahms and Schoenberg. In his last decades Stravinsky collaborated intermittently with scholars' discoveries, to help revise many people's "horizons" of the art. A continuity from Monteverdi to Dallapiccola, Berio, and others seems firmer now than in the 1930s, thanks partly to Stravinsky's *Orpheus* and *Rake's Progress,* as well as to the expansion of musicology. Gesualdo is no longer a freak, thanks partly to Stravinsky's *Monumentum,* alongside the work of Glenn Watkins and other scholars. Many of Stravinsky's works from the Mass through *Agon* to the orchestrations of the Wolf songs show his widening horizons and his contributions to the promoting of diverse fortunate continuities.

The continuity from Bach to Brahms and Berg and Babbitt need not be privileged with the metaphor of "mainstream." By 1967 Stravinsky declared that the "disappearance of a mainstream" was the chief fact of twentieth-century music.[3] Donald Tovey had already pictured the mainstream debouching into the ocean of Wagner.[4] By 1982, if Stravinsky had lived his full century, he would probably have abandoned this metaphor altogether. His translators in the *Poetics* (p. 77) used it for his explanation of his opera *Mavra* (1923): this work "stays within the tradition of Glinka and Dargomyzhsky. I had not the slightest intention of re-

2. Richard Taruskin mentioned this to the author in a private conversation.

3. Preface to *Storia della musica, vol. ix; la musica contemporanea* (Milano 1967); then in Stravinsky and Craft, *Retrospectives and Conclusions* (New York, 1969), p. 103.

4. "The Main Stream of Music," a lecture at the British Academy, 1938, was published in Tovey's *Essays and Lectures* (London: Oxford University Press, 1949), pp. 330–52; see particularly pp. 350–51 on Wagner.

establishing this tradition. . . . But I wanted to renew the style . . . a tradition that continued to live apart from the mainstream of the present [*tradition qui continuait à vivre en marge du présent*]." Let us emphasize that continuities and renewals in the margins can be fortunate. Perhaps some of these are more fortunate than one that has been clung to as central, as established forever, especially when it includes Wagner, as it must.

Persistent defenders of a musical mainstream in the twentieth century have placed Stravinsky's *Rite of Spring* in that stream; if they admit also *Petrushka* and *Les noces,* they are likely still to blame him for deviating to a margin in *Mavra.* About most of his works the persistent mainstreamers disagree among each other. Some critics regard almost everything from *Pulcinella* to the *Rake* as frantically discontinuous. Some see the same works as a stubborn, futile attempt to restore a broken continuity. Some others discern an esoteric continuity from the *Rite* through the Symphony of Psalms to *Agon* or *Threni* or the Variations in memory of Huxley, deprecating other works. Still others find Stravinsky closest to their mainstream in *Histoire du soldat, Rag-time,* and *Ebony Concerto.* A few Soviet ideologists claim a special central place for *Perséphone,* as fortunately continuous with the *Rite* and all sorts of earlier spring songs.[5] My glancing survey of these widely diverging views may be enough to dismiss them or to defer indefinitely any settlement of their divergencies. If their adherents want to view most of Stravinsky "in the margin," they may take comfort in agreeing to that extent with each other.

Yet Stravinsky has also attracted devotees in each generation through his long life who ranked him with the "great beacon-fires" and hence wanted to interpret his whole work as "promoting a continuity" that they could help to establish or reestablish. These devotees have disagreed among each other so far, as much as do the more selective critics. They find continuities for Stravinsky, by way of Debussy or Schoenberg or neither or both. And again by way of Britten or Stockhausen or neither or both. Such obscure continuities have not yet been traced in detail, though the evidence for them is accumulating. Are we ready in 1982 to coordinate such evidence? I doubt it. We need at least some dozens of investigators to weigh it, piece by piece, without partisan concern for any supposed mainstream.

Historians, theorists, critics, and others concerned to trace continuities can benefit by keeping in mind Stravinsky's plural and his adjective "fortunate." The loss of any particular continuity need not be deplored if the "sense of continuity" is not utterly lost. And no particular "freak" need be ostracized in our efforts to continue. What must be resisted is the tendency to "control the world" and to offer an "erratic block" as the "only model offered to students for emulation." For any individual, a fortunate continuity requires using several models, searching out

5. Boris Iarustovskii, *Igor Stravinskii: kratkii ocherk zhizni i tvorchestva* (Moscow, 1963), pp. 175–79. The German translation (Berlin, 1966) shortens the discussion of *Perséphone,* pp. 110–12, by several passages that show the author's fondness for the work. A more careful judgment is that of Mikhail Druskin, *Igor Stravinskii: lichnost', tvorchestvo, vzgliady* (Leningrad, 1974), p. 121: *Perséphone* is a "hymn to compassion," not always successful. The German translation of Druskin (Leipzig, 1976) is faithful, p. 140. Likewise the English (Cambridge, 1983), p. 97.

possibilities of connecting them with one's own ever-changing taste. Historians participate in the search for continuities, but if they pretend to control other people's searches then they may damage a true sense of continuity. This much seems to me implied in Stravinsky's words. It seems consistent with his whole work and with all he said and wrote throughout his life.

Stravinsky's eighty-nine years, viewed from a distance of eleven more, compose themselves a fortunate continuity. From the imperial theater of Saint Petersburg in the late 1890s to the White House, the Vatican, and the Kremlin in the early 1960s, the continuity was amazing—no simple straight line, no broad highway, but a unique streak of luck. No other individual enjoyed such a set of connections, by way of any peculiar route. Perhaps in some views of world history the ghastly accidents of wars, the transformations of sciences, technologies, and everyday styles of life, even the population explosion, may all seem subordinate to Stravinsky's good luck in upholding the values of creative art through so much of his frightful century, particularly in representing the prestige value of new art for social and political authorities and their lackeys. At the same time, in other views, Stravinsky's luck in evading so much of mankind's torment may be seen as limiting his work and its relevance for us and our possible posterity. His fortunate continuity, still, is something to be grateful for, no matter how marginal we estimate it.

Sheer continuity of the Stravinsky genes is less interesting than social continuities. It was less interesting to Igor Fyodorovich, as it is to us who celebrate his birth. But we may well take a moment to recall that Fyodor Ignatievich did not contribute to Igor's creative evolution as much as he was equipped to do. Did father and son ever make music together? Did Igor hear his father practice, rehearse with fellow singers, learn his roles, argue with directors? Could Fedor's great library or his friendship with the critic Stasov compensate for a strange discontinuity in the relationship? Biographers may uncover facts that Igor preferred not to discuss, which could help us understand his character and eventually his works. For now, just to note the intimate discontinuity can add a poignant connotation to the idea of fortunate continuities.

Stravinsky participated in many currents of artistic continuity without fully representing any one of them. As a Russian composer between Tchaikovsky and Shchedrin—or, if you prefer, Ustvolskaya or Denisov—he is important but not so representative of continuity as Prokofiev or Shostakovich. His connections with other nations have less to do with Russian power, political inspiration, and hope than those of Rachmaninoff or Scriabin or the Armenian Khachaturian. His biggest single work, *The Rake's Progress,* may contain some detectable debts to

Russian orthodoxy, to Tchaikovsky's *Queen of Spades,* to Pushkin and Dostoevsky, but these debts are inconspicuous, whereas strands connecting the *Rake* with eighteenth-century England, Italy, and Austria, and with twentieth-century New York, Hollywood, and Berlin, are relatively easy to trace, though few people would claim that Stravinsky was a leading representative of such strands. If *Mavra* should ever win repertory status, then the whole continuity of the Russian arts in the world would be immensely enhanced, but such a possibility seems farfetched, as Stravinsky well knew. He seems never again, after *Mavra,* to have projected or even dreamed of any work for a Russian stage, nor of finding music for the poetry of Pasternak, Akhmatova, or Mandelstam. I think he sensed that even Pushkin would always be marginal for most of mankind, that indeed Shakespeare and Racine were marginal, Goethe and Dante and Homer too, that all cultures were obsolescent in the world of atomic fission and TV. Like Eliot and Auden, he reaffirmed continuities that he could honestly choose, out of loyalty and study. He helped some people renew the musics of Bach and Mozart, if these people were willing to choose them freely, not merely to accept them smugly or to enforce an imperialistic worship of them. I think he knew that any culture is activity and sensitivity, rather than a national treasury.

In the world history of theater and dance, Stravinsky again participated without controlling or leading the way or representing any group. The extent of his work for ballet may be regarded as a legitimate accident of finances. He never foresaw it. He never allowed it to stop his tenacious efforts for opera and other more adventurous combinations of speech and song with instrumental music. *Histoire du soldat,* of all these works the one that exerted most influence on playwrights and producers, came about through the rupture of continuities, through legitimate accidents. *Histoire* is discontinuous with the fortunate line from Petipa through Nijinsky to Balanchine. Its connections with various later works are divergent. Stravinsky's most distinctive ballet, *Les noces,* remains in theaters an esoteric freak not yet accepted by many audiences as fulfilling the development from *Firebird* to *Petrushka* to the *Rite.* The fortunate continuity of those three most famous works is now appreciated by more people than can tolerate the exotic singing and the austere instrumentation of *Les noces,* despite the devoted revivals. Stravinsky's later combinations of dance and chorus and other elements, in *Perséphone* and *The Flood,* have won less success so far than *Les noces.* On the other hand, his further commission from Diaghilev, *Pulcinella,* seems to break continuity as much as to resume it. No matter how much *Pulcinella* may be enjoyed, esteemed, remembered, and even imitated, it hinders all perception of a continuous unfolding in Stravinsky's work as a whole. Moreover, though in fact *Pulcinella* is connected with some earlier commissions from Diaghilev to other composers, as well as with many other arrangements, it hardly contributes to a sense of continuity among such works. Does anyone claim a continuity from *Pulcinella* through *Le baiser de la fée* and *Jeu de cartes* to the fashions of the 1960s and '70s for surprising combinations of old and new styles? If anyone does, it is his personal claim. Is there any convincing account of continuity from *Pulcinella* through *Apollo* and *Orpheus* to *Agon* that does not invoke deeper, more elusive, more personal continuities, stretching back as far as *Petrushka*? No, the three ballets associated with Balanchine do not constitute a unit like the three early ones for Diaghilev. If *Agon* fulfills many continuous developments, these need to be studied throughout a vast range of works; any connection with *Pulcinella* needs to detach that work from Diaghilev and fashions, to fit it into the deeper, longer, personal continuities. But for now these remarks may suffice to indicate the intricacy of continuities and accidents in Stravinsky's relation to theater and dance.

The world of instrumental concert music has spread the ballets beyond theaters, but this world has not yet incorporated the work that Stravinsky offered it into its own fragile continuity as well as the theater has done with *Agon,* or indeed with the Violin Concerto, the Symphony in C, all favorites of the New York City Ballet in 1982. This paradox introduces my probing what seem to me important limitations on Stravinsky's achievement as a whole.

Did he recognize the historical relations between concert life and theaters? Did he ever extend his view of history and geography enough to see how rare is an audience that pays attention to structures of sound and silence and time, apart from narratives, characters, scenes, and conflicts of identifiable groups or interests? Did he invest naïve hopes in the possible public continuity from Beethoven through Liszt, Brahms, and Debussy to works like his symphonies, concertos, and Movements for Piano and Orchestra? Did he know that he might find more persistent perceptive listeners to his *Ebony Concerto* than to "Dumbarton Oaks"? When he chose forms and various types of the "polarity" (p. 52) or the "rotations" that he insisted would serve form, did his choices reflect any sense of concrete historical function for instrumental music, or did he entrust his hopes more to a transcendent enduring creativity? Did his choices of instrumentation, in the Symphonies for Winds, the Octet, the Septet, reflect an unforeseen trend to confine serious new instrumental music into a kind of academic chamber or ghetto? He was probably too busy to give these questions any sustained thought. His participation in concert life, though considerable enough to stir envy among many composers, was only sporadic, less closely connected with his inventions than was his teamwork in theaters. Moreover, I am not sure how often he achieved coherence in nontheatrical instrumental music. My uncertainty may be my own shortcoming, not his, but I attribute some of mine to the performers who have not yet played the music enough. Consider the Octet and the Septet: the Octet has gradually through many performances proved its coherence and its unique position in history, while the Septet still has patches that sound to me experimental—whether the performers are behind my imagination, or whether Stravinsky was venturing beyond the point where his imagination was sure is the issue. Since I need the continuity that the Septet has lacked, I raise the question whether Stravinsky needed it. If the question must remain unanswered, the fact remains that Stravinsky enjoyed more continuity in theaters than in concerts.

The long historical continuities of concert music and theater music both feed on the longer continuity of church music, shabby as this may often be. Stravinsky wished for a renewal of that great continuity, knowing it was unlikely. He wanted his Mass to function in a liturgy, to help believers. Likewise his earlier Credo and Pater Noster and Ave Maria. Probably the *Requiem Canticles*. Probably the anthem, *The Dove Descending*. Possibly *Threni*. His *Canticum sacrum* fitted the basilica of Saint Mark. His *Abraham and Isaac* was a tribute to hopes for renewal in Israel. Many other works depend on their religious texts to help shape the music. But each work is unique. His Mass has found fewer liturgical uses than Bach's or Beethoven's, far fewer than those of the Catholics Haydn and Mozart, or the Orthodox Bortniansky, Tchaikovsky, Rachmaninoff. With some of the works between the Mass and the *Requiem*, my position is just as it is for the Septet. Thus I think I imagine the *Dove* satisfying me deeply, but I can't be sure until I can work on it with a devoted chorus, more skillful than the ones I have recruited among students and more attuned to T. S. Eliot than the recording artists. The continuity I need here would be fortunate indeed.

In all the loose institutional continuities—of churches, theaters, concerts, schools—Stravinsky participated almost by accident. He was lucky to have as many opportunities as he did; we are unlucky that he lacked many he imagined; perhaps both he and we are unlucky in further lacks.

His lack sometimes drove him to indignation, often to spiteful uses of his wit and learning. In the 1930s, as he testifies in both the *Chronicles* and the *Poetics,* he was feeling that lack keenly. It seemed to him that he was increasingly frustrated by the culture that was "losing the sense of continuity." He confessed that from 1910 to 1914 he had been somewhat "spoiled" by public acclaim. Now he was misunderstood and estranged. He doubted that his early successes had meant any genuine communion. He recalled his loneliness and frustration in childhood and adolescence. So he insisted on his honesty, his diligence, his urgent need for order. He minimized the novelty of the *Rite of Spring*. He exaggerated the novelty of *Parsifal* and refused to see continuities in which Wagner participated. He despised Richard Strauss and seemed to ignore Gustav Mahler. When he bowed respectfully to Arnold Schoenberg, he made it clear that this was a distant respect, unlike the adoration he felt for his masters, including Tchaikovsky, or the enthusiasm and delight of his collaborations with Diaghilev, Nijinsky, Ramuz, Picasso, and other contemporaries, or even the gratitude he felt toward some conductors. He probably found no time in later decades to look for continuities in Schoenberg's development or Berg's, Webern's, Krenek's. When he became interested in some of their music and techniques, as Milton Babbitt has demonstrated, he picked out what suited his taste now, what could inspire him to make surprising continuities of his own, just as he had always picked what he liked from the "scattered things" (p. 32) of the past.[6] Toward other composers, including Carl Orff, Aaron Copland, Messiaen, Britten, and Stockhausen, he continued, with Robert Craft, to exercise his malicious wordplay, never inquiring about their diverse continuities. Historians must be skeptical of all he said, remembering that he wished he could erase it all. But at the same time, historians can use his words to help increase understanding of his music. Remembering how he prized the "tenacity" of Diaghilev, even when it led to quarrels, we may suppose that he would approve our using his words as legitimate accidents in our own searches for continuities.

6. Milton Babbitt, "Stravinsky's Verticals and Schoenberg's Diagonals: A Twist of Fate", in this volume.

The distinctive qualities of Stravinsky's music emerged gradually, from *Firebird* to the *Rite,* especially from the dance of Kashchei's demons to the "Great Sacrifice." This is the continuity that thrilled perceptive contemporaries and goes on winning more and more tenacious admirers and students. This continuity still needs definition and explanation, as far as these are possible. The distinctiveness unites techniques and purposes. Thus the peculiar rhythms embody extraordinary energy, not in any easy continuous momentum but rather in some sort of terrific conflict. In *Firebird* the conflict is clear, between utter malignancy and innocent youth; it is resolved at last by magic, by fortunate gifts, not earned. But already the conflict is Stravinsky's own, more intense than anything the dancers or audiences of 1910 had known. In *Petrushka* the protagonist has to suffer more than does the prince in the *Firebird* and his mocking survival at the end is not a triumph over the mean showman or the fickle public. This conflict is more distinctively Stravinsky's, as are the technical means that embody it, reducing *tempo rubato* to a minimum. In the *Rite,* the close-knit community watches its willing scapegoat dance to exhaustion; whether the sacrifice wins the favor of the gods is left for us to decide. Again, the vivid enactment of the pagan ritual in the virtuoso orchestra is Stravinsky's, sur-

Example 1: Igor Stravinsky, *The Firebird*.

Example 2: Igor Stravinsky, *Petrushka.* Copyright by Edition Russe de Musique. Copyright assigned to Boosey & Hawkes, Inc. Revised Copyright 1947, 1948 by Boosey & Hawkes, Inc; renewed 1975. Reprinted by permission of Boosey & Hawkes, Inc.

Example 3: Igor Stravinsky, *Le Sacre du printemps (Rite of Spring)*. Copyright 1921 by Edition Russe de Musique. Copyright assigned 1947 to Boosey & Hawkes, Inc. Reprinted by permission of Boosey & Hawkes, Inc.

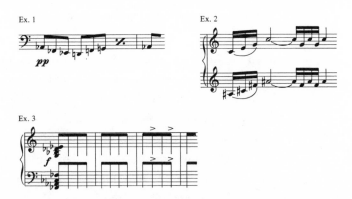

7. "Debussy, Stravinsky, and the Ballets Russes: The Emergence of a New Musical Logic," dissertation, the University of Chicago, 1981, University Microfilms 8113813; "Stravinsky's Visualization of Music; the Choreography of the Rite," *Dance Magazine* (April 1981), pp. 66–69; "Debussy, *Jeux;* Playing with Time and Form," *19th Century Music* 6/1 (Summer 1982):60–75; "Stravinsky and the Apaches," *MT,* 123 (1982):403–7.

passing any account by ecstatic poets and dancers, much more any painter's analogy or scholar's analysis, though collaborations of all of these may be indispensable.

Not only the crescendo of rhythmic novelty, but also the crescendo of dissonant intervals and challenges to all complacent reliance on diatonic scales belongs to Stravinsky's emergent distinctiveness. His pitch organizations are also embodiments of the increasingly distinctive dramatic conflicts. The mottoes of the three ballets are enough, for listeners fairly familiar with them, to make vivid what I mean (exx. 1–3). In these mottoes and their uses, I discern a kind of progress from abstraction and versatility toward a new concretion of pitch with timing and sonority, which fits the dramaturgy of the three works. This progress is not yet much commented on. Jann Pasler's work[7] has helped me try to think further about it. I believe that Stravinsky was aware of it, but never able to formulate his discoveries in words better than he did in the *Poetics,* lesson 2, when he said that "the articulations of musical discourse betray a hidden correlation between the tempo and the interplay of tones [*une correlation occulte entre le* tempo *et le jeu tonal*]" (p. 48).

With respect to forms, there is a fabulous tightening, served by the correlated tempi and play of tones. *Firebird* is assembled out of excerptible dances and meandering passages for mime, with the motto used discreetly to yoke things together. *Petrushka*'s mimes and dances interrupt each other and reflect each other, with the motto always attached to the central conflict. The *Rite* almost dispenses with mime; its two introductions surpass all static scene-painting and lead powerfully into the series of dances that seem to require each other, relentlessly.

Yet in every respect the fortunate continuity is confirmed by legitimate accidents. *Petrushka*'s rhythms and pitches often fall back from the novelty of Kashchei and the magic motto, not into the sweetness of the Khorovod or the Lullaby but into the deliberately banal waltz and the insistent C-major scale of the Russian dance. *Petrushka* relies on scene and character to make its forms satisfying in their vast expansion from the idea of a concert piece, which was Stravinsky's starting point for this work. The *Rite* veers off from *Petrushka*'s complexity and modernist loneliness; it romanticizes an exotic primitivism that Stravinsky did not adhere to. It suggests to many people a revolt against bourgeois assumptions and hopes that Stravinsky never thoroughly considered. The very suggestion embarrassed him long before the *Chronicles* and *Poetics*. The *Rite* is as freakish as anything by Berlioz.

A closer look at the chronological continuity from *Firebird* to *Rite*, if not yet so close as may be possible in the future, reveals many interruptions. Between 1910 and 1913, while the big project of the *Nightingale* was set aside, other short works were completed: two Verlaine songs, the setting for men's chorus and orchestra of Balmont's poem *Zvezdoliki*, and the orchestration of parts of Mussorgsky's opera *Khovanshchina*. The Verlaine songs seemed like trifles, throwbacks. *Zvezdoliki* appeared to the few who saw the score such a freak that it waited decades for performance and decades more for scholarly efforts to fit it into some kind of continuity with the Symphony of Psalms and later works. Moreover, the three ballets themselves overlapped. Before *Firebird* was completed, Stravinsky had told his collaborators about his vivid vision of the *Rite*. Before he and they had worked four months assembling materials for it, he was distracted by the inspiration of what became *Petrushka;* the collaborators went on to complete it while the *Rite* waited. What luck! Before the *Rite*'s first performance, postponed a year after the composing was almost finished (and thus anticipated impatiently by the best members of the elite audience), Stravinsky had begun his Japanese Lyrics and the group of friends had begun to discuss what finally, after the vast interruption of the war and after *Pulcinella*'s new shock, was presented to the public as *Les noces*. To trace chronological details, day by day when the documents make this possible, fascinates dozens of students of compositional process today. Our interpretations of the music can be affected by new knowledge of such details. Sometimes older interpretations can be refuted. Yet some of these may have engendered their own continuities, also worthy of study, no matter whether they are deemed fortunate or otherwise.

Continuities of both composition and interpretation interest me especially—continuities and accidents in their intricate complementarity. I have already indicated my interest with respect to the Septet and other later works (pp. 8–9 above). The collaborations of 1910–14 provided a continuity of performances that deserves recognition as extraordinary. This continuity, not just in Paris but on the road all over the capitals of Europe, fed into Stravinsky's composing. Did he then or later fully recognize what luck he had? Did he and others suppose that such continuity could be taken as a "general rule" rather than an "exception" in the twentieth century? Successful work in the theater had always involved some considerable continuity in collaboration, with composers hearing their new work learned by heart, repeated as part of a repertory, analyzed in rehearsals, applauded or hissed or yawned at by diverse audiences, often in several halls, several cities. Substituting individual performers, conductors, and assistants could be fortunate or unfortunate. In either case it could help composers refine their crafts to levels far above any academic prize mastery. Stravinsky learned his own kinds of orchestration and theatrical timing of instrumental music in the way Mozart and Puccini learned theirs. Did he recognize the limits of his luck in relation to theirs? On the basis of his "spoiling" experience in those four years he could feel deprived in later decades. He could also notice that most serious composers in his generation and later were likewise deprived, when considered by the standards of the *belle époque*. He could see some composers resigned to their lack, even some unaware of it in the age of phonograph and radio. But further, did he notice that even his luckiest years lacked the continuous experience with singers that Mozart and Puccini grew up with? experience that the heroic Richard Strauss acquired late, with *Salome* and *Elektra*? Did Stravinsky observe what a few younger composers managed to learn in their arduous continuous collaborations with singers—Poulenc or Eisler or Britten? Has anyone observed Stravinsky's lack of this kind of continuity? Is the time ripe for qualified people to study all Stravinsky's vocal music, his imagination of singing, in relation to his supreme confidence with instruments? His demands on singers in relation to his search for the "hidden correlation between the tempo and the interplay of tones?" My questions are too many! But, if any of my thoughts about continuities and accidents are remembered, I trust that these open questions will be among them, to extend some continuity into Stravinsky's second century.

As the second century begins, there are marvelous enterprises under way, seeking continuities of many kinds in Stravinsky's work and its influence. While I have emphasized here the work of 1910–13 that is most widely loved and recognized as continuous, I am impatient to find more continuities in the later works I love and those I still puzzle over. I am excited when I read in Paul Johnson's analytical thesis that he is on the track of what he calls a "continuous, methodical refinement of techniques, and a constant broadening of scope" in Stravinsky's works from 1918 to 1951, *Histoire* to the *Rake*.[8] I anticipate continuous help from Richard Taruskin as his studies proceed from the *Rite* to *Histoire* and on into the 1920s, combining theoretical acuity with unique qualifications as a historian.[9] Further collaborations of historians and theorists, lately tempted more and more to stray from each other as well as from performers, seem to me necessary for the "true evolution of culture"

8. "The First Movement of Stravinsky's *Symphony in C*: Its Syntactical Bases and Their Implications," dissertation, Princeton University, 1981, University Microfilms 81214771, p. 6; pp. 91–125.

9. See especially his article in this book.

and for cumulative public truth even within specialized disciplines that treat such "hidden correlations" as Stravinsky's.

Continuity and accident are among the themes of the second lesson in the *Poetics*. In describing his creative process Stravinsky exalts continuities and gives a subordinate but essential place to accidents. Possibly my dwelling on these themes facilitates a review of the famous description. Stravinsky asserts that creators of art continuously exercise their appetite, continuously practice their craft, and continuously refine their taste through culture. The gift for creating is inseparable from a gift for observing accidents, which may be the only source of inspiration, as they present obstacles to any routine application of learned rules of craft and thus renew appetite. Likewise, an inventor's new works, outrunning rules of craft, eventually renew tradition and assure the continuity of creation, of culture.

This account might have been clearer and more persuasive if Stravinsky had thought to qualify the continuities here with the word "fortunate" as he did in the later lecture.

The account is rather obscured by his bitter condemnation of common images: creators inspired by inner feelings, following caprices of imagination or fantasy, soaring above craftmanship, usurping the authority of rulers, priests, and enlightened patrons. Stravinsky asserts his own humility with such defiant dogmatism that he accidentally hides his genuine humility and betrays some lack of the assurance that he claims. Could he have regarded the common images as legitimate accidents?

Since he denounced them as illegitimate, his *Poetics* has failed, so far, to renew his cherished continuity of culture. For many readers it rather contributes a bit to the chaos that Stravinsky hates. But for persistent students, even his failure may provide the accidental obstacle that renews an appetite to "participate actively in the working of a mind that orders, gives life, and creates" (p. 28).

Stravinsky's VERTICALS AND SCHOENBERG'S DIAGONALS: A TWIST OF FATE

MILTON BABBITT | *Princeton University*

When a prime mover and shaper of this conference induced the specific title and general content of this paper by reminding me of an almost forgotten remark, years ago dropped in class, as to the remarkable relation between Schoenberg's diagonals (as I viewed them) and Stravinsky's verticals (as he viewed them) by a rotation which transforms—symmetrically—one into the other, he did so but a few days before I was asked to speak on what soon became "Order, Symmetry and Centricity in Late Stravinsky" delivered at the International Stravinsky Symposium held (September 12–14, 1982) at the University of California, San Diego. Although I realized I could not avoid an intersection of content, I foresaw little conflict of interests. For, since the Symposium hoped to invoke the commemorative, celebrative, and—where pertinent—the personal, at the Conference I resolved to maintain a properly ascetic academic posture by pursuing immediately, impersonally, and unswervingly the technicalities entailed by the title. But for all of their dual geneses, the papers necessarily shared their source, their musical motivation: that single work which remains the most fascinatingly perplexing and refractory of Stravinsky's compositions, and the one which he clearly and dramatically regarded as decisively different from all that had preceded and as decisively influential on all that followed. In his own words: "The slow climb through the 1950's eventually brought me to the *Movements,* which I now see as the cornerstone of my later work."[1] "I have discovered new (to me) serial combinations in the *Movements* for piano and orchestra . . . the most advanced music from the point of view of construction of anything I have composed. . . . Every aspect of the composition was guided by serial forms, the sixes, quadrilaterals, triangles, etc. The fifth movement, for instance, . . . uses a construction of twelve verticals."[2] And I could continue to heap hyperbole upon Stravinsky's sometimes elliptic descrip-

1. Igor Stravinsky and Robert Craft, *Themes and Episodes* (New York: Alfred A. Knopf, 1966), p. 23

2. Igor Stravinsky and Robert Craft, *Memories and Commentaries* (New York: Doubleday and Company, 1960), p. 100.

tion, but—instead—I shall yield to the temptation to reminisce, but only twice, and then only with explicative respect to the Movements, of which I first became aware in December 1958, when Stravinsky came to New York to conduct the first performance of *Threni*. Mrs. Stravinsky, Robert Craft, and I were sitting in the living room of the Stravinsky suite at the Gladstone Hotel, waiting for Stravinsky to join us for dinner; he was in the bedroom, doing we knew not what, but the suspicion that he was composing his new work for piano and orchestra was verified when, suddenly, he emerged, in his robe, waving a sheet of manuscript paper, smiling that familiar pixy-like smile, and shouting: "I found a mistake, and the right note sounds so much better!" Among the lovely resonances of this remark is its illumination of Stravinsky's assertion later, at the time of the *Requiem Canticles,* that he continued "to follow the logic of his ear,"[3] particularly for those who are wont to emphasize the rhetorical use of "ear" at the expense of the metaphorical use of "logic." And as for those who seize upon the statement to intimate that the music is less "out of ear" than "out of mind," let them—instead—contemplate Stravinsky's mode of affirming that the "ear" is at least as theory laden as the eye and mind, and that only the mind's ear and the ear's mind can provide the now so necessary sorting, selecting, and censoring.

3. *Themes and Episodes,* p. 23.

Stravinsky devoted a year to the twelve-minute Movements, and on the morning of January 9, 1960, he conducted the final rehearsal for its first, so to speak, performance. We, many of us, lunched, and then—either because or in spite of the quality and quantity of the luncheon wine not having been ordinary—Stravinsky insisted that Claudio Spies and I escort him down the street from the Ambassador Hotel, the luncheon scene, to the Gladstone Hotel, where—again—the Stravinskys were staying. There he further insisted that we accompany him to their suite, where he produced *all* of his notes, alphanumerical as well as musical, pertaining to the Movements, and proceeded, as if to restore for himself and convey to us his original, unsullied (by actual, approximate performance) image of his creation, a creation that clearly meant crucially much to him.

I do not know how long his exegesis lasted, but I vividly recall that dusk arrived, and we scarcely could follow him visually on his charted voyage of rediscovery, but we dared not turn on a light for fear it would interrupt the flow of his discourse and the course of his thought. But I doubt that it would have, for he did not drop a syllable of whatever language he was speaking at that moment when I, in a spontaneous burst of détente, observed that the hexachord of the Movements was the same as that of Schoenberg's *De Profundis*. If I do not recall when that extraordinary seminar ended, I surely do not remember how, but I do know how and for how long Claudio Spies and I have tried to reconstruct that journey through the composition, or precomposition.

The next evening, there was the first, so to speak, performance of the Movements, and in the accompanying program notes Stravinsky revealed it all: the hexachords, the verticals, the series as viewed through a not so metaphorical "crystal." The secrets were out, and in. And seventeen years later, those revelatory notes still could evoke outraged cries from a violated dilettante, who angrily called them "more like a chemical formula" and "claptrap," and—with the calm, considered understanding characteristic of his considerable clan—suggested the assistance of an "astrological chart" for the "average music lover."[4]

In person, and through his program notes and subsequent written statements, Stravinsky left no doubt as to what the Movements and the notions of musical structure embodied and exemplified in it meant to him; I propose to attempt to suggest something of what it meant in and to his music, and to music.

However Stravinsky arrived at the "new combinations" and procedures of the Movements, they produced novel consequences by a formally single operation upon or transformation of a, by now, traditional way of viewing the Schoenbergian instigated and employed twelve-tone syntax. The set (or "series" or "row") of the Movements—dispositionally, functionally defined by precedence and weight of presence and reference—is placed, seriated—from left to right representing the order numbers for 0–11 inclusive—as the first row of such a familiar 12-by-12 array (ex. 1a). From just the two premises of such an imposed linear ordering and the intervallic determination of "chromatic" distance between pitch classes, the total array can be constructed, for the first row (usually the, or an analytically, contextually arrived-at twelve pitch-class set) can be regarded as a succession of interval measurements from the first element (the element whose order number is 0), and the remaining rows (from top to bottom) are derived by considering the successive pitch classes as successive origins of such measurement, to the "right" and "left." The successive rows are then successive transpositions, at transposition levels complementary (mod. 12) to the p.c. number (in the "original" first row) of the new origin, the zero of the row in question. Thus, of course, the successive columns of the array are the familiar inversions, at successive transposition levels defined by the initial set. The retrograde and retrograde inversion set forms are then derivable by applying the same sequence of operations to order numbers, that is—what amounts to complementing them mod. 11. But the crucial formations for this discussion are the resultant diagonals; the main left to right diagonal, the successive origins, can be viewed as presenting the interval between each successive

4. Neil Tierney, *The Unknown Country* (London: Robert Hall Ltd., 1977), pp. 175–76.

Example 1a

0	1	7	5	6	11	9	8	10	3	4	2
11	0	6	4	5	10	8	7	9	2	3	1
5	6	0	10	11	4	2	1	3	8	9	7
7	8	2	0	1	6	4	3	5	10	11	9
6	7	1	11	0	5	3	2	4	9	10	8
1	2	8	6	7	0	10	9	11	4	5	3

3	4	10	8	9	2	0	11	1	6	7	5
4	5	11	9	10	3	1	0	2	7	8	6
2	3	9	7	8	1	11	10	0	5	6	4
9	10	4	2	3	8	6	5	7	0	1	11
8	9	3	1	2	7	5	4	6	11	0	10
10	11	5	3	4	9	7	6	8	1	2	0

pitch class of the set and itself, or—equivalently—the pitch-class interval between elements whose order number interval is 0. Then, the next diagonal to the right presents the successive intervals defined by pitch classes whose order number interval is 1, what is customarily called the set's interval series. The next diagonal to the right presents the intervals created by pitch classes whose order number interval is 2 (that is, which are separated by a pitch class). And so on. (The complete verticals are obtained, obviously, by replicating and concatenating the array.)[5]

By simply aligning these diagonals as verticals, or—equivalently—rotating the array to achieve this deployment of the diagonals, a Stravinskyan array results.[6] His most characteristic method, that of operating upon the two discrete hexachords separately, yields from the array of example 1a that of example 1b. The dislocation of the order of the transpositional rows of the second hexachord, as opposed to the preservation of the order of those of the first hexachord, is an immediate indication of the new affinities induced by the slightly whirled series, for all that the derivation of the 6-by-6 array of the second hexachord is by strict analogy with or—perhaps better—from the structure, but not from *our* derivation, of the first hexachord.

To describe, without other reference or origin, the successive rows of the first hexachord of example 1b as derived by "rotation" is not only to appear to invoke a

5. For a fuller discussion see my article "Since Schoenberg," *Perspectives of New Music* 12, nos. 1–2 (1973–74):25–27.

6. This relation and the general subject of order transposition are discussed in Charles Wuorinen, *Simple Composition* (New York and London: Longman, 1979), pp. 101–9.

Example 1b

0	1	7	5	6	11	9	8	10	3	4	2
0	6	4	5	10	11	9	11	4	5	3	10
0	10	11	4	5	6	9	2	3	1	8	7
0	1	6	7	8	2	9	10	8	3	2	4
0	5	6	7	1	11	9	7	2	1	3	8
0	1	2	8	6	7	9	4	3	5	10	11

deviant, "arbitrary" manipulation, but to obscure and deflect those attributes which bind the array to the past and recent past of music and of Stravinsky, as well as to the basic relations of serialism. If, however, the array is characterized as a collection of transpositions, whose order and size are determined by the referential set, both the historical and systematic associations are made more vivid and potent; I even dare suggest that it was such a construal that led Stravinsky to discover or have uncovered for him the congeries of relations and interconnections which appear suddenly and so intricately in Movements. But I do not dare suggest that he knew or cared that the canonic relation which obtains among the transpositionally related lines of the array, the "structural" imitations, were—at least—adumbrated by Wagner, and celebrated by Schoenberg, most pertinently in his Op. 16, No. 3, where, although Schoenberg's underlying five-part canon was both a pitch (not merely pitch-class) and rhythmic canon in the traditional sense, for all its imitational explicitness its primary effect seems to have been to project the resultant "chords," "simultaneities," "verticals," so decisively that one of the titles imposed on the movement is "The Changing Chord." And the chord that is changed is yet another point of consilience between that work and Stravinsky's "new combinations." And the canonic structure of the array is but a special case of that contextually determined "motivic" voice-leading polyphony in which the constituent lines derive and create their coherence from and by their direct transformational, intervallic dependence upon one another rather than as tokens of types of formations and progressions derived from the same context-independent structure.

The "verticals," the columns formed by elements standing in the same order position in the six transpositions of the array, have no predecessors in serial or preserial composition, but they do have—if only attitudinally—predecessors in Russian music: in Rimsky (in the harmonic "theory" and the compositional practice) and—of course—in Scriabin and after, where the "chord" is regarded more as a thing-in-itself, a collection, even as a spatial and temporal ordering of pitches, than in its tonally functional role. The "chord" as compositional premise, as sonorous object, as "tonic sonority," as generative source was not exclusively Slavic, and Stravinsky's "verticals" stand in a different hierarchical position, as consequences rather than as antecedents, but the conceptual resemblance is unmistakable, and the relations necessarily induced by the successive transpositions are generalized instances of the notion of associative harmony, which is just "contextually coherent" harmony. And it is just these chordal verticals which most significantly and characteristically distinguish Stravinsky's use of the transposed lines from Krenek's. There is evidence that Stravinsky knew Krenek's *Lamentations of Jeremiah*[7] and, even, that Krenek expounded to Stravinsky the methods of the

7. Igor Stravinsky and Robert Craft, *Dialogues and a Diary* (New York: Doubleday and Company, 1963), p. 52.

work. But Krenek's primary view and use of the transpositions of the hexachords were as "modes," never compounded into such an array as could yield the "verticals" and the multitude of other suggested configurations and paths through the total hexachordal and set complex.

I risk redundancy in reiterating that this transpositional generation of the array discloses the singular role of transposition (itself, as we have observed, derivable from the assumption of "interval") in twelve-tone serialism, particularly as an operation—taken together with the linear ordering entailed by the very term "serial"—which produces inversion, which is—accordingly—a "supervenient," whatever had been its direct, suggestive genesis as a motivic operation on contour, obscuring its much more general character as an operation of complementation. And this "Sheffer stroke" of the twelve-tone syntax when applied to order number, produces "rotation." For example, the successive lines of example 1b can be produced by applying to the ordered couples—of order number, pitch-class number—of each of the elements of the first hexachord, the successive transpositional couples (0,0); (5,11); (4,5); (3,7); (2,6); (1,1). (The operational analogy with the comparable application of complementation to the components of the couple—producing the "retrograde inversion"—is not inconsequential.)

As a consolidated extension of his own compositional ontogeny, Stravinsky's arriving at novel procedures rooted in the "interval" surprised no one who knew works as seemingly remote from the Movements as, say the Capriccio, the Symphony in C, the *Jeu de cartes,* for, in Stravinsky's own words, he always had "composed with intervals." But this assertion itself incorporated a not universal perception of the "interval" as the central, irreducible determinant of the constancies and invariants of twelve-tone structure, and may reflect the hindsight provided by arrays, which in pitch-class and interval content, are supersaturated by the influence of the interval structure of the initial hexachords, for since each vertical is, under the rotation of the "Schoenbergian" array, a prerotational diagonal, each vertical is determined by the successive pitch-class intervals of each successive order number interval; that is, every interval of the hexachord, not just successive intervals, affects the content of every vertical, including its pitch-class multiplicity. The intervals created by the pitch-class components of the verticals are, then, intervals of intervals, the differences between interval sizes in the original series. This apparently "theoretical" relation, whose compositional function and influence are scarcely explicit—or even latent—in the traditional 12-by-12 representation, becomes a foreground constituent. In the Movements, an interval (and, of necessity, its complement) not present in the original hexachordal *collection*—the interval 3, or 9—appears immediately as an adjacency-defined interval in the second and third verticals, and—therefore—necessarily (though not necessarily defined by a literal adjacency) in the sixth and fifth verticals. It is such immediate properties of directly derived verticals, so dissimilar from those of the initial series which—alone—may make the composition appear, that is "sound," so "hermetic," as it has been described by a Stravinsky biographer. As the listener engages in the familiar epistemic act of acquiring knowledge and remembered knowledge of a work as it proceeds, the bases of interconnection, of cumulative continuity may seem so unfamiliar as process, perhaps so tenuous, that—with no putative "form" worn on the composition's sleeve—the network of associations, however multiply reinforced, powerfully transitive, and subtly redundant, is ultimately dependent, as the vehicle of coherence, on the very pace of the transformational process, which is the critical temporal, "rhythmic" control of the work, particularly since Stravinsky's method is so extremely sensitive to order, to pitch order, as a primary boundary condition. The minimal change in the order of the pitch elements of the initial hexachord, such as the interchange of the positions of two adjacent elements, will, in general, alter violently the structure of, not just those verticals of which the elements are immediate constituents, but of all the verticals. (I trust it is unnecessary to add the modification that the first vertical is excepted, by definition of the procedure.) In example 2 the last two elements of the hexachord have been interchanged; the resulting verticals bear no reasonable relation to those of example 1b, not even the gross number of different pitch classes present matches in all cases. This is not to suggest that Stravinsky ever engages in such a procedure, but it is strongly to suggest the care which had to be expended on the ordering of the initial series in order to secure a given, desired collection of verticals. And the extent of that awareness easily can be observed in the set of the Movements. It already has been noted that there is no interval of 3 (or 9) in the initial hexachords; therefore there can be no pitch class 3 or 9 in the 6-by-6 array generated by the first hexachord. (Since each hexachordal line starts from 0, the presence of pitch class 3 or 9 would thereby represent an interval of 3 or 9 in the hexachord; the interval number, p.c. duality strikes again.) Therefore, Stravinsky chose 9 as the first element of the second hexachord and so obtained a complete equality of p.c. multiplicities within the two 6-by-6 arrays of the two hexachords. That is, each pitch class occurs exactly six times, whereas if he had chosen, say, 8 as the first element of the second hexachord (a useful ploy: the placing of a hexachordally excluded interval at the joint of the hexachords), then there would be no such balance. Further, but independently, the final elements of the two initial hexachords (11 and 2) also were chosen to create the missing interval 3, so that the retrograde generated arrays would possess the same characteristic. The inversions of the prime and retrograde arrays necessarily preserve this property, which is highly contextual, the consequence of a particular ordering of a set which belongs to a special subclass of a special class of sets (second-order all-combinatorial). But it is a general, systematic property of the operation that the successive transpositions it induces, at the transpositional levels identified by the t numbers standing to the left of the first 6-by-6 array in example 3a, yield the initial hexachord of the first column of the conventional 12-by-12 array, that is, the inversion of the first hexachord (reading the t numbers as p.c. numbers), and the second hexachord's 6-by-6 array similarly produces the inversion of the second hexachord at the transposition level 9.

If one can, as one must, take seriously Stravinsky's often orally expressed discomfort with the notion (more accurately, the slogan), "the identification of the horizontal and the vertical," one must, first of all, regret that he permitted himself to be affected by this admittedly widespread misunderstanding of Schoenberg, who, even if he ever expressed it in quite that verbal manner, was not prescribing some automatic identity or permitting whatever goes up to go sideways, but describing modes of deriving, from the materials of single line, the criteria for polyphonic combination of lines, themselves transformations of the referential single line. In any case, Stravinsky wished a basis of differentiation of the vertical and horizontal dimensions comparable, at least in structural force, with the tonal distinction between the triad as the norm of the vertical and the scale as the archetype of the horizontal. And surely his "search for new combinations" brought him, in the structural distinctions between his sets and his verticals derived from them, such a differentiation. Yet he not only came to apply various local techniques to secure whatever identity was possible between his verticals and their horizontal origin (in the opening measures of the Variations—for instance—by removing those pitches of the verticals which violated such an identification and appending them as grace notes, as Jerome Kohl has shown in his valuable study)[8] but the identity it built—subtly but solidly—into his transformational procedure, since the successive elements of each vertical are successive elements of the original series, each transposed by—again—the complements of the successive elements of the original "horizontal."

8. Jerome Kohl, "Exposition in Stravinsky's Orchestral Variations," *Perspectives of New Music* 18, nos. 1–2 (1979–80):391–405.

Example 2

0	1	7	5	11	6
0	6	4	10	5	11
0	10	4	11	5	6
0	6	1	7	8	2
0	7	1	2	8	6
0	6	7	1	11	5

Example 3

		H₁						H₂						
	t = 0	0	1	7	5	6	11	9	8	10	3	4	2	0
	11	0	6	4	5	10	11	9	11	4	5	3	10	1
	5	0	10	11	4	5	6	9	2	3	1	8	7	11
S	7	0	1	6	7	8	2	9	10	8	3	2	4	6
	6	0	5	6	7	1	11	9	7	2	1	3	8	5
	1	0	1	2	8	6	7	9	4	3	5	10	11	7
	0	0	11	5	7	6	1	3	4	2	9	8	10	0
	1	0	6	8	7	2	1	3	1	8	7	9	2	11
	7	0	2	1	8	7	6	3	10	9	11	4	5	1
I	5	0	11	6	5	4	10	3	2	4	9	10	8	6
	6	0	7	6	5	11	1	3	5	10	11	9	4	7
	11	0	11	10	4	6	5	3	8	9	7	2	1	5
	0	11	6	5	7	1	0	2	4	3	10	8	9	0
	5	11	10	0	6	5	4	2	1	8	6	7	0	10
	6	11	1	7	6	5	0	2	9	7	8	1	3	11
R	4	11	5	4	3	10	9	2	0	1	6	8	7	4
	10	11	10	9	4	3	5	2	3	8	10	9	4	6
	11	11	10	5	4	6	0	2	7	9	8	3	1	5
	0	1	6	7	5	11	0	10	8	9	2	4	3	0
	7	1	2	0	6	7	8	10	11	4	6	5	0	2
	6	1	11	5	6	7	0	10	3	5	4	11	9	1
RI	8	1	7	8	9	2	3	10	0	11	6	4	5	8
	2	1	2	3	8	9	7	10	9	4	2	3	8	6
	1	1	2	7	8	6	0	10	5	3	4	9	11	7
	3	3	4	10	8	9	2	0	11	1	6	7	5	3
	2	3	9	7	8	1	2	0	2	7	8	6	1	4
	8	3	1	2	7	8	9	0	5	6	4	11	10	2
S	10	3	4	9	10	11	5	0	11	1	6	5	7	9
	9	3	8	9	10	4	2	0	10	5	4	6	11	8
	4	3	4	5	11	9	10	0	7	6	8	1	2	10
	9	9	8	2	4	3	10	0	1	11	6	5	7	9
	10	9	3	5	4	11	10	0	10	5	4	6	11	8
	4	9	11	10	5	4	3	0	7	6	8	1	2	10
I	2	9	8	3	2	1	7	0	1	11	6	7	5	3
	3	9	4	3	2	8	10	0	2	7	8	6	1	4
	8	9	8	7	1	3	2	0	5	6	4	11	10	2

A transposition of a hexachord does not, in general, induce a permutation of the hexachord. Only the whole-tone collection yields six permutations of itself under Stravinsky's transpositional procedure; the hexachords of the *Movements* are permuted under $t = 6$ because of their second-order structure. So, the hierarchical criteria applicable among these transpositions are the traditional ones of degree of pitch intersection, rather than the strictly serial and more problematical criteria of degrees of differences among orderings, which Schoenberg resolved by identity of hexachordal content between differently ordered sets. But the novel result of Stravinsky's transformation of the two hexachords by the same operation but "independently" is that the "lines" created by the concatenation of the two disjunct hexachords are not necessarily (and most often cannot be) aggregates, since the series of transposition numbers associated with the two hexachords are, in general, different and—even—different in content. In the case of the Movements, the two hexachordal collections are transpositions of one another, and—therefore—the two series of transposition numbers are permutations of each other, reflecting the differences of *ordering* between the two hexachords. So a new criterion of affinity and new paths of associations are created, which Stravinsky exposes early in the Movements. In measures 13–17 (ex. 4), the progression from the piano through the clarinets moves linearly through the second hexachord of the second line of example 3, where $t = 1$, then the first hexachord of the same line, where $t = 11$, followed by the second hexachord of $t = 11$ (on line 3 of ex. 3); with the final B♭ of this last hexachord as "pivot," the progression is retrograded to the "A" of the bass clarinet (in measure 17) with the "expected" E♭ (corresponding to the "E♭" of the piano in measure 14) appearing in the piano in measure 18, as a means of pitch connection between apparently "disconnected" sections. In passing, it should be noted that the unique grace-note A♭ in the piano in measure 13 may possess its notational singularity (in this passage) to signal a dislocation of order, although I suspect it is an erroneous transcription from the manuscript. More consequential is the G♭–D♭ of the clarinet in measures 13–14; the notes are doublings of the piano and bass clarinet notes, respectively, and are the only such doublings in the passage, maintaining the emphasis on that pitch dyad which had been established in measures 2 (as an adjacency of the work's set), 4, 6 (both in the strings and the piano), and 12! This is a characteristic means of local association, but the progression through the three hexachords, in which the second is a link between a linear association and a transpositional association, is a process which is central to this and the later works of Stravinsky. The second pair of these hexachords necessarily creates an aggregate (but not a set form in the traditional sense, because of the alterations of order created by Stravinsky's procedure); the first pair produces a "doubling" of the elements of the symmetrical tetrachord 4, 5, 10, 11 (indeed, a second-order tetrachord) while the remaining, "unique" pitch classes are 0, 3, 6, 9, whose particular relation to this set and piece is obvious.

Example 4: Igor Stravinsky, Movements for Piano and Orchestra. Copyright 1960 by Hawkes & Son (London) Ltd. Reprinted by permission of Boosey & Hawkes, Inc.

Milton Babbitt

Ex. 4 (cont.)

Ex. 4 (cont.)

9. Robert Craft, *Stravinsky: The Chronicle of a Friendship* (London: Victor Gollancz Ltd., 1972), pp. 85–86.

10. Eric Walter White, *Stravinsky the Composer and His Works* (Berkeley and Los Angeles: University of California Press, 1966), pp. 464–66.

The appearance of a passage like that beginning in measure 13 so early in the work may be one of the sources of the work's appearing largely impenetrable and "hermetic." For, although Stravinsky appears to have shared with Schoenberg a taste for a phanic, foreground statement of the set at the outset of a work, very soon (in the Movements by measure 3) it recedes to exert its pervasive, persistent influence, acting and interacting at ever varying distances from the musical surface, to reappear explicitly at such points of articulation as the end of the first movement and the end of the work, and, in all its "forms" hexachordally partitioned, after the double bar ending the body of the fourth movement (mm. 137–140), presumably an instance of that added "minute or two."[9] There are other passages, particularly in later works, which may seem even more dependent (and less musically "logical") on the deployment of the various 6-by-6, 6-by-12, etc. arrays of example 3, and so even suggest that the musical paths are visually patterned unto synaesthesia, but none of those cases is musically more remote than, say, the right-to-left main diagonal in the S-array of the first hexachord in example 3, yielding 11, 10, 4, 6, 5, 0, which is simply the familiar inversion (at $t = 11$), for as "Schoenberg's" diagonals are Stravinsky's verticals, so are Stravinsky's diagonals "Schoenberg's" verticals; the relation, like so much to come, is symmetrical.

The celebrated polyphonic fellow (in the flute) of the passage beginning in measure 13 is now so comprehensible as to require only a mention of the "minor third (B flat followed by G natural)"[10] which the commentator who termed the Movements "one of the most hermetic of all Stravinsky's major works" characterized as an instance of the "one or two unorganised notes that seem to serve as passing notes" since the interval is "foreign to the series." It is not, however, foreign to the third vertical derived from the first hexachord, or the sixth vertical derived from the second, etc.

Since Stravinsky's "new discoveries" so extensively depend upon the two hexachords acting independently, and so relatively rarely do transformations of the complete initial set appear, there may arise the question as to the significance of the total set, as opposed to the constituent hexachords. But just because they are complementary hexachords, by the "hexachord theorem" they—uniquely—have the same total interval content (importantly including intervallic multiplicity). Therefore they stand in the same hierarchical pitch-class content relation to their corresponding transpositions, to their transpositions even as transformed by "rotation," since the interval content of the hexachords is independent of order; it is a property of the hexachords as collections.

What particularly surprised and delighted Stravinsky was the discovery that the variety the verticals introduced with respect to the referential set was counter-

11. See my "Contemporary Music Composition and Music Theory as Contemporary Intellectual History," in *Perspectives in New Music*, ed. Brook, Downes, and van Solkema (New York: W. W. Norton & Co., 1972), pp. 166–67. But a thorough investigation of the properties of the array of verticals and its extensions can be found in a series of articles by John Rogers: "Toward a System of Rotational Arrays," *American Society of University Composers Proceedings of the Second Annual Conference* (April 1967), pp. 61–74; "Some Properties of Non-Duplicating Rotational Arrays," *Perspectives of New Music* (Fall–Winter 1968), pp. 80–102.

balanced by the now most familiar of their systematic properties: the unities among them, the symmetries.[11] That the verticals symmetrically disposed about the center vertical (the initial vertical of 0's is disregarded) or—equivalently—that the verticals whose order numbers are complementary mod. 6 are inversionally equivalent, and—therefore—that the center vertical is internally (inversionally) symmetrical is but another instance of the inversional identity of retrogression and inversion; here, the retrogression of the rows induces the inversional relation among the columns. The concept of a symmetrically constructed chord, or simultaneity, or vertical is not visual or quasi-geometrical; it describes patterned intervallic redundancy. The five-part chord of Schoenberg's Op. 16, No. 3, as intimated above, is symmetrical; the symmetry is created by the expansion of the transposed opening trichord motive of the whole work (b–c–e) by its conjunction with its inversion (a–g♯–e), with the thus created symmetry "e" compositionally noted and exploited as such, while the canonic theme of the movement is itself symmetrical around its first note.

Further, the I 6-by-6 array of the first hexachord—whether arrived at by direct substitution of complements in the S-arrays, or by transpositional generation from the I-form of the set—contains verticals which are, in exact pitch content (and altered in internal order only by a displacement according to a simple pattern), the reverse in order of those in the S-array. Naturally, in the case of the second hexachords, the same relation holds to within the transpositional difference between the two hexachords, in this case 6. Therefore, the middle verticals are identical in content in the case of the first hexachords, and to within transposition between those of second hexachords. So inversion of the set induces retrogression of verticals as retrogression of p.c.'s induced inversional relations among the verticals, relating, thereby, all of the verticals associated with all four "standard" transformations of the set.

These systematic properties of symmetry yield even closer identities under special properties of the set. In the Movements, the *ordering* of the second hexachord is such that the two discrete trichords are inversions, in order, of one another; therefore, in the second hexachord generated array, symmetrically placed verticals are not just inversionally symmetrical but identical in content. And they would not have been had the trichords been transpositions (as they can be in such a second-order set); here, an inversional relation yields a simpler, "stronger" similitude than the "simpler" operation of transpositions.

But symmetry defines and requires a center of symmetry. The pitch-class center for all the verticals is the initial p.c. of the hexachords. This p.c., then, is distinguished not just by virtue of primacy and multiplicity but as the referent of symmetry. In the Movements, consider the role of the E♭, in the *Requiem Canticles* the F, with which the work begins and ends.

Again, the past is recaptured and enhanced. A half-century ago, we heard that Stravinsky was fond of declaring that his Piano Concerto was not "in A," but "on A," that the pitch class "A" was not tonic, but centric (this latter formulation is, probably, not his), and the centricity was established by a variety of means of emphasis and reinforcement, of which conventional procedures of triadic tonality were but instances, and then used only locally and occasionally, if strategically and influentially. In his new cosmos, pitch-class centricity is the compositional point of convergence for all the symmetries, and is so projected compositionally by an even greater lexicon of means. A characteristic example can be observed in m. 40, where the structurally centric E♭ is emphasized subtly and transitorily by the contrapuntal relation between the flute and bass clarinet—bassoon lines, where the pitch class E♭, and only that pitch class is "doubled." Even a taxonomic study of the multitude of means of establishing and maintaining the inceptually centric pitch class would be profitable and revealing.

When Stravinsky spoke, again elliptically, of the "hint of serialism" in the rhythmic structure of the Movements, which he did not discuss further except to characterize it as his "most advanced," which is obvious on the very surface of the Movements and the Variations (the only two purely instrumental late works), and not just the linear rhythms are unprecedentedly varied and intricate, but—and this almost follows—the ensemble rhythms, which Stravinsky said were "meant to be heard vertically." This suggests an affinity between the "array" of linear rhythms and the "array" of hexachordal transpositions. The serial aspect is not apparent in any but a loosely analogical sense, and in the nonsense of nonrepetition, which is a manifestation of serialism only by guilty association with that old prescriptive chestnut which confused the structure of a set with its contextual interpretations, and produced a "principle" which corresponded to no composition. But there are "new" modes of temporal organization more or less coordinated with or motivated by the serialism of pitch structure; the function of the barline or the measure at— for example—the opening of the work, where the first measure contains the set's first hexachord, ending with a "d," and the second contains the second hexachord, ended with an (isolated) "f"; the third measure begins by collecting these two notes, which—as already has been pointed out too frequently—cannot be adjacent in any set form, but which introduce the functions of recollection and overlap this early in the work. The statement of the set in the opening two measures can be viewed as partitioned into 5 + 7, particularly in view of the instrumental partitioning of the pitch-class literal retrograde at the opening of the last movement, while the three simultaneous "E♭'s" of the fourth sixteenth of the first beat of the work correspond to the three successive "E♭'s" of measure 3, etc. etc.

As for the "suggestions of serialism" in the instrumental structure of the Movements, hexachordal completion already has been observed in the connection between instrumentally disjunct measures 17 and 18; when in measure 40 the viola states a low "g" pizzicato and the second pitch of the hexachord to follow, the first pitch of the hexachord ("f") had been stated in measure 21 (pizzicato and registrally adjacent to the "g" of measure 40); between those two points, the only pitches stated by the viola are in 35–36, all in the instrument's upper register, *arco sul ponticello*. In measure 137 the expected "a" of the clarinet (ex. 5), expected by its immediate "doubling" with the bass clarinet and bassoon, and its role as the first element of the second hexachord, occurs as the first note of the clarinet in the following movement (measure 143). Again, the *Tristan* prelude recalled, as in the first bassoon between measures 11 and 16. Here too, the nonrecurring character of the instrumental combinations[12] may have seemed "serial" to Stravinsky, but they also suggest, particularly when considered in the light of the pitch connectives between separated and disjunct sections, a construal of the work in terms of sliced and intercalated continuities and consecution which suggest an uninterrupted continuity in Stravinsky's methodical progress, a strong similarity with the processes Edward Cone discovered and illuminated in his study of "middle-period" works.[13]

The Movements is a special work in all the ways Stravinsky observed and, beyond those, in its set's structure and its consequences. His last large composition, *Requiem Canticles,* reveals two sets, whose appearances are symmetrically distributed around the Interlude, the centerpiece of the main body of the work, where

12. Milton Babbitt, "Remarks on the Recent Stravinsky," in *Perspectives on Schoenberg and Stravinsky* (revised edition), ed. Boretz and Cone (New York: W. W. Norton and Co., 1972), p. 182. Reprinted from *Perspectives of New Music* 2, no. 2:35ff.

13. Edward T. Cone, "Stravinsky: The Progress of a Method," in *Perspectives on Schoenberg and Stravinsky,* pp. 155–64. Reprinted from *Perspectives of New Music* 1, no. 1:18ff.

Example 5: Igor Stravinsky,
Movements for Piano and
Orchestra. Copyright 1960 by
Hawkes & Son (London)
Ltd. Reprinted by permission
of Boosey & Hawkes, Inc.

32

Ex. 5 (cont.)

V

14. For a thorough discussion of all aspects of this composition, see Claudio Spies, "Some Notes on Stravinsky's Requiem Settings," in *Perspectives on Schoenberg and Stravinsky,* pp. 223–49. Reprinted from *Perspectives of New Music* 5, no. 2:98ff.

the two sets both appear, and simultaneously once, at the center of the centerpiece.[14] The two sets' internal structures are decisively different (see ex. 6); the second set is inversionally combinatorial (the two hexachords are collectional inversions of one another); the first is not. But the two sets share an attribute attributable to the "new combinations" which is a determinant of their parallel structuring; whereas in the Movements the *t*-values induced by the successive transpositions were the same for both hexachords, this is not the case for the hexachords of the *Canticles;* but both of the dissimilar sets yield transposition series for the two hexachords which have four numbers in common, therefore, which make available four possible lines by aggregate formation. (Not incidentally, the transposition numbers in common—in both cases—when interpreted as p.c. numbers, yield all-combinatorial tetrachords: 0, 5, 6, 7 and 10, 11, 0, 1.)

Example 6

Requiem Canticles

		H₁						H₂						
	t = 0	0	7	6	4	5	9	8	10	3	1	11	2	0
	5	0	11	9	10	2	5	8	1	11	9	0	6	10
	6	0	10	11	3	6	1	8	6	4	7	1	3	5
S	8	0	1	5	8	3	2	8	6	9	3	5	10	7
	7	0	4	7	2	1	11	8	11	5	7	0	10	9
	3	0	3	10	9	7	8	8	2	4	9	7	5	6
	0	0	5	6	8	7	3	4	2	9	11	1	10	0
	7	0	1	3	2	10	7	4	11	1	3	0	6	2
	6	0	2	1	9	6	11	4	6	8	5	11	9	7
I	4	0	11	7	4	9	10	4	6	3	9	7	2	5
	5	0	8	5	10	11	1	4	1	7	5	0	2	3
	9	0	9	2	3	5	4	4	10	8	3	5	7	6

		H₁						H₂						
	t = 0	0	2	10	11	1	8	6	7	9	4	3	5	0
	10	0	8	9	11	6	10	6	8	3	2	4	5	11
	2	0	1	3	10	2	4	6	1	0	2	3	4	9
S	1	0	2	9	1	3	11	6	5	7	8	9	11	2
	11	0	7	11	1	9	10	6	8	9	10	0	7	3
	4	0	4	6	2	3	5	6	7	8	10	5	4	1
	0	0	10	2	1	11	4	6	5	3	8	9	7	0
	2	0	4	3	1	6	2	6	4	9	10	8	7	1
	10	0	11	9	2	10	8	6	11	0	10	9	8	3
I	11	0	10	3	11	9	1	6	7	5	4	3	1	10
	1	0	5	1	11	3	2	6	4	3	2	0	5	9
	8	0	8	6	10	9	7	6	5	4	2	7	8	11

One afternoon in the summer of 1962 at Santa Fe, when Stravinsky's birthday was being celebrated, he was taken to see and hear works by the young composers imported for the occasion. On the way back from that meeting, he observed quietly and perhaps slightly sadly, with insight and foresight, that those composers would not possibly be interested in what he was now composing; he had just begun *Abraham and Isaac.* Rather, he thought, they would return to his *Firebird,* or—even more likely—to his *Fireworks.* But there have been the fortunate few who not only have been interested in those last works but have found in them the bases of yet newer combinations, further and personal extensions. Among these are the varying periodicities created by a chain of verticals, and the regeneration of verticals. Unlike the traditional twelve-tone transformations which are all of periodicity 2, or the transpositions, limited to the periodicity defined by the transposition number, the successive application of verticalization creates intricate and extended structures of periodicity. In example 7 the second vertical of example 3 generates a 6-by-6 array; the second vertical here has more different pitch classes than the original second vertical; so does the middle vertical expand its content. Repetitions in a hexachord, one sees, do not yield necessarily repetitions in the verticals because of the difference in order numbers of the repeated pitch classes. Each of the verticals changes, regenerates, and is enriched in its own way, following its own path toward its future where it, too, can seek and find "new combinations."

Example 7

1	6	10	1	5	1
1	5	8	0	8	8
1	4	8	4	4	9
1	5	1	1	6	10
1	9	9	2	6	9
1	1	6	10	1	5

PROBLEMS OF HIERARCHY IN *Stravinsky's* OCTET

ETHAN HAIMO | *University of Notre Dame*

Some idea of the extent of the conceptual problems posed by Stravinsky's "centric music" can be gauged from the number of markedly different theoretical approaches that have been advanced to explain this repertoire.[1] Some of the earliest writers, noting both the superficial similarities with tonal practice and the evident divergence from that practice, suggested a number of terms (bitonality, pantonality, modality, pandiatonicism) that they felt might capture the essence of the Stravinsky style.[2] In an attempt to account for the seemingly stable function of nontriadic elements, Travis postulated the existence of a referential sonority that substitutes for the tonic triad and that is articulated through time by techniques analogous to those of tonal music.[3] Boretz suggested that some pieces are best thought of as lacking a tonic and instead proposed that they be viewed in terms of a reference tetrachord or hexachord ("construct centric").[4] Still others (Salzer, Forte) extended Schenkerian analysis to include Stravinsky's works.[5] Berger and after him van den Toorn have directed attention to various collections that they portray

1. The term "centric" was applied by Berger to describe music that is "centric (i.e. organized in terms of a tone center) but not tonally functional." Arthur Berger, "Problems of Pitch Organization in Stravinsky," *Perspectives of New Music* 2 no. 1 (1963):11; reprinted in Boretz and Cone, eds., *Perspectives on Schoenberg and Stravinsky*, rev. ed. (New York: W. W. Norton, 1972), p. 123. Further citations are to the reprint.

2. Paul Collaer, *A History of Modern Music*, translated by Sally Abeles (New York: Grosset & Dunlap, 1961), pp. 137–39; Roman Vlad, *Stravinsky*, trans. Frederick, 3d ed. (London: Oxford University Press, 1978), pp. 12–18.

3. Roy Travis, "Toward a New Concept of Tonality?" *Journal of Music Theory* 3 (1959):257–66.

4. Benjamin Boretz, "Meta-Variations, Part IV: Analytic Fallout (II)," *Perspectives of New Music* 11, no. 2 (1973):167–75.

5. Allen Forte, *Contemporary Tone Structures* (New York: Columbia University Press, 1955), pp. 128–38 and 187–92; Felix Salzer, *Structural Hearing* (New York: Dover, 1962), vol. 2, pp. 234–37. Travis, pp. 257–66, employs Schenkerian reductions.

6. Berger, "Problems," pp. 124–44; Peter van den Toorn, "Some Characteristics of Stravinsky's Diatonic Music," *Perspectives of New Music* 14, no. 1 (1975):104–38 and 15, no. 2 (1977):58–95. The ideas in these articles were much expanded in van den Toorn, *The Music of Igor Stravinsky* (New Haven: Yale University Press, 1983).

7. Paul Johnson, "The First Movement of Stravinsky's Symphony in C: Its Syntactical Bases and Their Implications," dissertation, Princeton University, 1981, pp. 25–33.

8. Allen Forte, *The Harmonic Organization of "The Rite of Spring,"* (New Haven: Yale University Press, 1978); Joseph Straus, "A Principle of Voice Leading in the Music of Stravinsky," *Music Theory Spectrum* 4 (1982):106–25; Charles Joseph, "Structural Coherence in Stravinsky's *Piano Rag Music*," *Music Theory Spectrum* 4 (1982):76–91.

9. There are substantial disagreements between many of the authors cited. See for example van den Toorn, *The Music of Igor Stravinsky*, pp. xiv–xv.

10. Travis, "Toward a New Concept," pp. 257–66, deals with Stravinsky in the context of an attempt to arrive at a new concept of tonality that would embrace this music as well as other styles.

11. Salzer, *Structural Hearing*, pp. 234–37; Forte, *Contemporary Tone Structures*, pp. 128–38 and 187–92.

12. Berger, p. 131.

13. Berger deals with many issues of hierarchy: see pp. 130–38 in particular, although this is an issue running through

(continued)

as basic to many of Stravinsky's works. Those collections (diatonic, octatonic, and octatonic/diatonic) are ordered and partitioned in various ways.[6] Another writer (Johnson) has suggested a different collection (0123578t) as basic to much of Stravinsky's output. He also discussed ways in which this collection is partitioned and how it functions over an extended span.[7] Finally, a number of attempts have been made to apply atonal set theory to Stravinsky's works.[8]

One of the reasons that it has been so difficult to come to terms with Stravinsky's work may be the very diversity of the music. *The Rite of Spring* and the Octet are by the same composer and were written within fifteen years of one another, but their stylistic differences are substantial. Perhaps no single theoretical approach could provide meaningful insights into the systematic organization of works of such distinctive styles.[9]

Similarities with tonal music have created other problems for theorists. Since we have a very thorough knowledge and understanding of tonal music, it has proved to be very difficult to approach Stravinsky's music without preconceptions conditioned by tonal theory. Indeed, all too often an understanding of the music of Stravinsky has suffered because of unfortunate and questionable comparisons made employing techniques and concepts of dubious applicability. Clearly we have to push beyond the stage of misapplying tonal theory and start to approach his music in its own right without being dependent on theories that were designed to explain another musical repertoire. At the same time we cannot automatically reject the possibility that there could well be real, not just superficial, connections with past procedures and that ideas borrowed from tonal theory could prove most useful.

Several of the studies cited above have invoked the concept of hierarchy and have sought to apply it appropriately to Stravinsky's music. Terms such as "referential sonority" and "nonfunctional" tonic were created in an attempt both to identify the centric quality of the music and to differentiate its hierarchical procedures from those found in tonal music.[10] The Schenkerians not only claim referential priority for a tonic (even for a tonic triad) but also, by their reductive procedures, claim that there are hierarchical distinctions between notes on the surface.[11] Informally, and sometimes even casually, theorists not committed to the Schenkerian view describe occasional notes as passing tones, neighbors, or appoggiaturas, thereby demonstrating a belief in different hierarchical levels.[12] With the exception of the Schenkerian approach these studies have not systematically approached the problem of hierarchy as a whole, as a series of interlocking relations.[13] Such a systematic examination is the object of the present study. The types of collections used, their specific pitch-class content, the presence or absence of local tonal centers, the

the entire discussion. Van den Toorn as well deals with aspects of this problem: see *The Music of Igor Stravinsky,* pp. 73–90, where there is much discussion of "pitch class priority."

14. Eric Walter White, *Stravinsky* (Berkeley and Los Angeles: University of California Press, 1966), pp. 275–76.

15. They stand at the same hierarchical level excepting tonic assignment. That will be discussed shortly.

16. Boretz, "Meta-Variations," p. 167.

existence of a global referential sonority (or tonic), the use of elaborative tones, and the syntax that would permit their identification all involve issues of hierarchy and will be treated here. However, instead of examining these as individual issues, they will be treated as related facets of an integrated compositional system.

As my point of departure, I would like to examine the first movement (the Sinfonia) of Stravinsky's Octet. This work is particularly suitable in that it is relatively straightforward and seemingly uncomplicated in its tonal and formal outlines. Furthermore, the changes between the now unavailable 1923 edition and the easily obtained 1945 revision are minimal.[14] Finally, the first movement, though certainly related to the remaining movements, is not so dependent on them for intelligibility that it would be meaningless to discuss it without reference to the others. Although my conclusions are going to be drawn from analytical observations and abstractions from the Octet, I do not feel that the theoretical formulations I am going to suggest are entirely unique to that piece. Rather, I would maintain that, in some form and to varying degrees, these aspects of Stravinsky's approach to structuring his material are also applicable to many of his neoclassical compositions.

§1

If a collection is defined by listing all pitch classes that occur, then a one-to-one correspondence is asserted between the observable pitch classes and membership in the collection. By implication, all the pitch classes would be viewed as standing on the same hierarchical level.[15] However, once the concept of hierarchy is invoked it cannot be assumed that any given pitch class is a member of the referential collection. Rather, membership in the collection must be tested in context. Given presuppositions inherited from experience with tonal music, there might be a tendency to presume a note to be part of the referential collection if it helps form one of the diatonic scales. Or, conversely, one might tend to consign a note to elaborative status if it does not fit into one of those scales. Both such presuppositions could be erroneous and could indicate a failure to view this music on its own terms.

A second problem involves the criteria that would permit the identification of a passage as a coherent unit with its pitch classes constituting the referential norm. Normally the pitch-class content is one of the principal criteria that permits us to identify coherent units of musical space.[16] Yet we cannot invoke this criterion at this stage without being guilty of circular reasoning.

Fortunately, there are sufficient examples of exceptional clarity that it is no great achievement to be able to identify coherent musical units and, from there,

17. Johnson, "The First Movement," pp. 25–33. This collection is formulated and described here but not given the name "eight-note diatonic collection." See Johnson's essay in this book for further discussion of the collection and its properties.

work backwards to an identification of their constituent pitch-class elements and from there to some simple conclusions about the kinds of collections employed.

The first thirty-four measures of the Allegro moderato (rehearsals 6–10) offer some straightforward examples. By invoking a number of quite simple criteria (motivic repetition and transposition, orchestration, dynamics, and so forth), it is clearly not only possible, but reasonable and musically sound to think of these measures in terms of seven distinct and coherent musical units. (I hesitate to use the term "phrase" because of its tonal implications.) Five of these form one of the twelve possible diatonic collections. The remaining two collections are extensions of the diatonic collection, the so-called eight-note diatonic collection (ex. 1).[17] The collection used in the fourth through sixth measures of rehearsal 8 is an instance of this collection (ex. 2).

Example 1

Measure	Collection	Name
♮6	C, D, E♭, F, G, A♭, B♭	E♭
♮7	C, D♭, D, E♭, F, G, A♭, B♭	E♭/A♭
♮8$^{1-3}$	C, D♭, E♭, F, G♭ A♭, B♭	D♭
♮8$^{4-6}$	C♯, D, D♯, E, F♯, G♯, A, B	E/A
♮8^{5}–♮9^{5}	C♯, D, E, F♯, G, A, B	B♭
♮9$^{6-7}$	C, D, E♭, F, G, A, B♭	G
♮10$^{1-5}$	C, D, E, F♯, G, A, B	

Any attempt to resolve this collection into a more traditional diatonic collection would be futile. Both the D and D♯ give every indication of being entirely stable tones; neither seems to be best thought of in terms of another, more stable tone. The D♯ in the A trumpet occurs as a result of a literal transposition of the motive from the preceding measure and will in turn be literally transposed three measures later. The D appears numerous times in these measures in different instruments with different kinds of treatment and similarly seems quite stable.

It should be noted that the D and D♯ do not appear freely intermingling, but that there is a partition of the elements such that D♯ appears only in the upper parts and D only in the lower. In other instances in the Octet where this collection type occurs similar treatment of the material is found, indicating that such a partitioning

Ethan Haimo

Example 2

of the elements may be a critical feature of the syntax. One way of conceptualizing this might be to consider that two separate diatonic collections are involved, E and A, collections with six common elements, partitioned into different registers. In turn, such a conceptualization might account for other collections found in the movement. For example, the passage comprising rehearsal 16, although there are other complications, might profitably be regarded as having G, B♭, and C collections partitioned into the different instruments (ex. 3).

Example 3: Igor Stravinsky, Octet for Winds. Copyright 1924 by Edition Russe de Musique; Renewed 1952. Copyright and renewal assigned to Boosey & Hawkes, Inc. Revised version copyright 1952 by Boosey & Hawkes, Inc. Renewed 1980. Reprinted by permission of Boosey & Hawkes, Inc.

Chromatic scale collections occur quite often and seem to fall into two categories. The type that can be reduced to a diatonic background will be treated in the next section of the paper as it involves issues of hierarchy. Equally common seem to be collections that are chromatic in which no diatonic collection could be inferred. Stravinsky does not freely move about in a chromatic texture in any way analogous

Example 4: Igor Stravinsky, Octet for Winds. Copyright 1924 by Edition Russe de Musique; Renewed 1952. Copyright and renewal assigned to Boosey & Hawkes, Inc. Revised version copyright 1952 by Boosey & Hawkes, Inc. Renewed 1980. Reprinted by permission of Boosey & Hawkes, Inc.

Example 5

to Schoenberg. Rather, the lines, either simply (ex. 4), or by implication (ex. 5), proceed directly through chromatic scale segments in such a manner that differentiation of the pitch classes into hierarchical levels is difficult and thus reduction to a simpler background impossible.

§II

The collections identified so far have included all the pitch classes of the sections in which they appear. If we were to persist in identifying collections only in terms of the specific surface content, we would continually be forced to invoke new collectional types to account for the pitch material of this movement. However, if we introduce the concept of hierarchy at this point and postulate that some notes might best be thought of as elaborations of the referential collection, then it would be possible for us to think of this movement in terms of a limited number of referential collections. Thus for a passage like example 6 I will suggest that not all the notes are members of the referential collection, but rather that the "A" is a passing tone. This would allow us to postulate two levels of meaning for the observable collection of this passage: a diatonic, referential collection would form one level and several elaborative tones would form the other.

The application of the concept of elaboration to this passage carries with it certain dangers. Even if it proves to be a valid and useful way of viewing the passage and others like it, we cannot accept it without challenging the assumptions that lie behind it, nor without proposing some rules of syntax specifically designed to explain this composition's patterns. Perhaps the simplest way to do this is by comparing the function of chromatic tones in tonal music with the function of those notes in the Octet that seem to have a similar function.

Example 6

passing tone?

In tonal music a chromatic tone is a dissonance, one that resolves to a stable tone, a diatonic note. This is true even where the chromatic tone is locally consonant. At the first level of reduction such tones clearly lose their consonant support and reveal themselves as dissonances: either neighbors or passing tones, but not as suspensions because a suspension must be introduced as a consonance, something clearly not possible for a noncollectional tone.

The problem with applying this kind of concept to the Octet and other diatonic pieces like it should be apparent: such an application is dependent on a contrapuntal theory that would demand clear definitions of consonance and dissonance. I feel fairly certain that no convincing case could be made for absolute function of dissonance in Stravinsky's works. Although it seems as if thirds, sixths, fifths, octaves, and unisons certainly act consonant all or most of the time, the rest of the intervals seem most chameleonlike. Sevenths for example sometimes seem to be unstable, tending to resolve to combinations contextually defined as stable. But other times sevenths act as if they are completely stable, seemingly needing no further clarification. Moreover, there is an added complication. Chromatic tones in tonal music are like vectors; they carry within themselves the direction they wish to resolve and they resolve there by half-step. In the process we tend to think of upward-resolving chromatic tones as implied leading tones and downward-moving ones as either resolving sevenths or suspensions. Just as much as it is misleading to talk in terms of consonance and dissonance underlying chromaticism in Stravinsky, so, too, leading tone function and seventh chord resolutions seem to be concepts inappropriate to a proper understanding of this style.

These negative assertions about chromaticism thus do not, of course, tell us what the functions of such tones could be in Stravinsky's works. To achieve that end I would like to propose some simple rules of syntax.

Let us consider the tones of a given referential diatonic or extended diatonic collection to be stable: they carry no implicit need for immediate motion to another, more stable tone. By contrast then, tones outside the given collection are understood to be unstable: they must resolve to a more stable element, a note from the referential collection. The resolving motion to a stable element must be by step, either half-step or whole step and will occur within a voice. (Note that the "vector" concept is absent.) The motion from a noncollectional tone must be by step, but the motion *to* that tone need not be. As a result two types of noncollectional elaborations are possible, passing tones and neighbors. (Incomplete neighbors and double neighbors are clearly possible.) Just as in tonal music, a voice may not appear explicitly on the surface but may be part of a compound line within an instrument. Thus a resolution of a noncollectional tone to a diatonic tone may not appear directly on the surface. It may appear as if the chromatic tone is skipped from, but, by the simple rules of syntax, it must be stepped from either directly or indirectly or it cannot be heard in terms of the referential tone. Example 6 shows such a situation.

These simple rules of syntax are easy to apply if, and only if, the referential collection is established unequivocally. The problem, of course, is that the very presence of noncollectional tones in a system with no consistent definition of consonance and dissonance can create confusion as to what exactly is the referential collection. For example, given a sequence of four tones, G, A♭, A, and B♭ as in example 6, how is it possible to determine which of these are from the referential collection and which are elaborative? Clearly, the only way it is possible to make such a determination is if one or several of these pitch classes have been previously established unequivocally, by these rules of syntax, as referential.

Using these rules of syntax it is possible to demonstrate that a number of passages, quite chromatic on the surface, have a simple diatonic referential framework. A good example of this is the Lento introduction of the first movement where everything up to rehearsal 4 can be related to a background E♭ collection.

§III

If the concept of hierarchy offers an efficient and effective means of assigning different levels to the elements of the observable collection, then, by logical corollary, we should consider the possibility of the application of this concept within the referential collection. That is, within these collections, does one pitch class receive referential priority? Can we talk about toniclike function in this piece? If so, how is it established?

Certainly, the fact of such referential priority has been claimed innumerable times in relation to Stravinsky's music. The titles of many of his works and some of his published statements indicate that Stravinsky himself considered one pitch class to have some sort of referential precedence. However, there are a number of problematic aspects to this concept.

On the local level, what are the criteria for stating that a given pitch class is the referential norm around which the other pitch classes gravitate? Certainly in tonal music such a situation obtains by means sufficiently sophisticated that the tonic can be established without actually being stated. In Stravinsky's works, in the absence of such functional relationships, it seems that the tonic must be determined by straightforward and perhaps necessarily simple insistence on the desired pitch class. This might involve orchestrational doubling and accent, repetition, agogic accent,

18. Berger, p. 126.

19. Van den Toorn, *The Music of Igor Stravinsky,* p. 80

metric emphasis, starting or ending point of melodic motion, centricity of melodic patterns, coincidence between voices, and much else besides. By such means tonics might articulate any one of seven possible referential orderings.[18]

On the global level a tonic cannot be articulated by such simple means. Rather, it must be established by contextual relationships between the various local tonics. An examination of this issue must therefore be deferred until later when we have more information about the piece as a whole.

Inasmuch as the specific identity of the tonic is not established *a priori* by the collection, so too it must be recognized that a tonic of any sort does not automatically result merely because the elements of the collection are stated. This is so particularly given that tonics are established not by functional relationships but rather by local emphasis. Thus I would assert that, in contrast to tonal music, a tonic is not a given in Stravinsky's diatonic music, and in particular in the Octet, and that it must be defined by the context, the possibility existing that a given passage could have *no* tonic.[19] For example, the first three bars of rehearsal 8 contain the seven pitch classes of the D♭ major collection, but if one pitch class were to be assigned referential priority in this passage it certainly is not the case that it would have to be D♭. (G♭ seems to be as strong a candidate.) The situation is sufficiently ambiguous that I maintain that it is unprofitable to postulate any tonic here (ex. 7).

Given the content of collections and the assignment of tonics as variables then, it is possible to create a complex matrix of possible relationships between two sections in this system. The closest kind of relationship, the identity, would have both tonic and collection common to two different sections. Closely related are sections in which the collections are identical but the tonic assigned to each is different. Yet another possibility is to have two different sections in which the tonic is held fixed while the collections change. Finally, even if the collection and tonic are different the referential ordering can be identical.

The establishment of a tonic does more than merely extract one pitch class from the rest of the collection in a hierarchical ranking. Rather, it determines the referential ordering of the collection. In this dimension there is greater differentiation possible than in tonal music. Given one diatonic collection, there are conceivably seven possible tonics and thus seven potential referential orderings, each with a characteristic and unique interval ordering. The possibility of a section having no tonic creates even more avenues for compositional exploitation and allows another set of variables to be employed in compositional decisions concerning the relationship of pitch material to large-scale structural function.

These observations about the existence, establishment, and function of refer-

Example 7: Igor Stravinsky, Octet for Winds. Copyright 1924 by Edition Russe de Musique; Renewed 1952. Copyright and renewal assigned to Boosey & Hawkes, Inc. Revised version copyright 1952 by Boosey & Hawkes, Inc. Renewed 1980. Reprinted by permission of Boosey & Hawkes, Inc.

ential tonics should prompt a number of difficult questions about hierarchy in addition to those that should arise from the earlier discussion about hierarchy of collections. Obviously, we want to know how tonics and collections established in the middle of a composition relate to the overall tonic of the piece. If we are to have an understanding of compositions like the Octet that goes beyond the mere identification of what changes where, then an attempt has to be made to relate the progression from a given area and tonic to the large-scale progression of the piece. We need to be able to show how the various disjunct tonics and collections relate to one another in an integrated manner, in a way that accounts for progression, not merely recounts succession.

§IV

On the most obvious and superficial level the Sinfonia clearly has parallels, if perhaps only metaphorically, with classical sonata form. The Lento section (rehearsals 1–5) acts much like a classical introduction section: the tonic collection, E♭, is stated from the beginning, and indeed, seems to be the referential collection though much elaborated, as far as rehearsal 4. Yet throughout, the tonic of the piece, E♭, is not established as referential at any point after the first measure and even there it is very weakly defined. Instead B♭ with D seem to be given some sort of referential priority from rehearsals 1–4. Commencing with rehearsal 4 are ten measures of great instability, both in terms of the rapid and complex changes of collection and also in that no pitch class seems to be singled out as having referential priority.

The opening of the Allegro moderato, at rehearsal 6, acts like an exposition. A clearly stated E♭ collection and tonic with a highly etched theme is followed by a move, from rehearsals 8–10 through a number of areas before arriving at a second theme with a D tonic and G collection, which is followed by the same theme with an A♭ tonic and a D♭ collection at rehearsal 12. A "development" section follows. It is highly unstable, avoiding both clear tonic assignment and a stable collection and lasts up until five measures before rehearsal 18 whereupon Stravinsky initiates a partial and backwards recapitulation, reintroducing various material from earlier and including two restatements of the second theme, one with an E tonic and the other with an E♭ tonic. This is followed at rehearsal 19 by an unstable passage, quite chromatic, which leads into a final restatement of the first theme with a clearly etched E♭ center.

These observations should permit some tentative conclusions about hierarchical function of collection and tonic establishment in this composition. It seems that it would be a useful and reasonable hypothesis to suggest a correspondence between stability and tonic-assigned diatonic collections on the one hand, and instability and tonicless chromaticism on the other. These should be regarded as the extremes of a sliding scale. Such a hypothesis, when tested against the superficial formal structure of this movement, seems to work quite well, and it would seem that it reflects on the large scale the nature of chromaticism that we have already seen as operative on the level of detail: noncollectional tones act like dissonances, needing to resolve; chromatic collections act unstable, moving toward points of greater structural stability, characterized by diatonic or extended diatonic collections.

Yet such a dynamic, however accurate and however neatly it supports the sonata form, remains incomplete unless the specific pitch content and exact tonic designation are taken into account. Without such a determination, we would be dealing with a theoretical hypothesis that would allow any pitch level anywhere. I feel certain that Stravinsky's specific pitch choice is not arbitrary nor would it permit recomposition at different levels without complete distortion. A determination of that level of tonal logic must be the next and final step up the hierarchical ladder.

§v

The Lento introduction sets the stage for and establishes the context of the progressions that control the harmonic structure of the movement as a whole. Up through rehearsal 4 the E♭ collection, even though almost buried at points by its elaborations, is still understandable as the referential collection. (Even around rehearsal 2, where the C collection briefly comes to the fore, the E♭ collection can still be heard as referential in the larger context.) The application of the rules of syntax discussed previously can clarify the compound lines that underlie the surface and show the eventual disposition of various noncollectional tones. (See ex. 8.) After that point, the number and degree of changes in collection are so rapid as to nearly suppress the E♭ collection, but even here it still is perceptible, particularly when one recognizes that some of the "resolutions" result from the transference of pitches from one instrument and register to another. For instance, the noncollectional neighbor to B♭, the A natural (second trombone, one before rehearsal 5), is transferred to the trumpet an octave higher in the next measure before it finally returns to a collectional B♭ just before the Allegro moderato. (See ex. 9.) At the same time that the E♭ collection is established as the referential collection of the introduction, Stravinsky fosters a certain ambiguity in terms of referential tonic. Although E♭ is stated in m. 1 with the support of its triad,[20] it is not retained or reiterated at important structural moments. Instead, most of the introduction seems to be best thought of in terms of the predominance of a B♭–D dyad. Throughout this section the bass line moves through a B♭–D range and at every articulative point D appears in the bass with

20. Berger, p. 127.

Example 8: Resolving non-collectional tones.

Symbols used: Open note = collection tone: Filled note = noncollectional tone:
                Dotted line = retained tone: Slur = path of resolution

Example 9: Octave transfer.
Igor Stravinsky, Octet for
Winds. Copyright 1924 by
Edition Russe de Musique;
Renewed 1952. Copyright and
renewal assigned to Boosey &
Hawkes, Inc. Revised version
copyright 1952 by Boosey &
Hawkes, Inc. Renewed 1980.
Reprinted by permission of
Boosey & Hawkes, Inc.

octave transfer

resolution

Example 10: Cadence
sonorities, introduction.

support of B♭ or A♭ with F or all three. (See ex. 10.) Certainly it is obvious that these "cadential" sonorities form what could be termed dominants, and one might be tempted to invoke tonal functionality here. However, I think that since we will see no other such atavistic tonal functionality and since there is no basis for thinking in terms of root progressions, it is best to treat these sonorities in terms of their specific quality merely as an historical reference.

If we are to sum up the tonal progression of the introduction, then we could describe it as an extended statement of the E♭ collection with a brief statement of the tonic in m. 1 followed by an extended suspension of E♭ tonic function, and with an unresolved dyad, D–B♭ repeated as the principal articulative sonority. In these terms then we can see the introduction as a prolonged tonal upbeat, setting the stage for the structural arrival that will be coincidental with clear tonic definition.

Such takes place clearly and undeniably with the opening of the Allegro moderato and the statement of the first theme. The collection is pure E♭, untinged by any chromaticism; the lines clearly gravitate around E♭ and no other pitch class could reasonably be offered as referential. Thus the extended tonal instability of the introduction is resolved here and we are presented with some of the fundamental characteristics of tonal meaning and definition in this piece. In the process the voice leading shows the nature of that tonal definition. The bass tone D moves to E♭ while the B♭ in the upper parts is retained as a common tone. Therefore the essential motion, a bass motion, is D to E♭ and this is how the tonic is defined.

Starting at rehearsal 7 there is a varied repetition of this opening, but a crucial difference appears. A D♭ appears, first in the bassoon but shortly elsewhere as well, and it neither displaces the D nor seems to meet our criteria for thinking of it as an elaborative tone. Thus we seem to have an eight-pitch class, extended diatonic collection, or a partitioning of the E♭ and A♭ collections. We might be tempted by habits from past repertoires to consider this collection as less stable than the simple E♭ diatonic collection. Such a bias would, however, lead to a misconstrual of function as the eight-element collection is in fact quite stable and is indeed the closing collection of the movement.

Starting at rehearsal 8 there is a sequential statement of the (altered) opening theme with a descending whole step as the interval of sequential repetition. This sets in motion several tonicless collections that settle down only at rehearsal 9 where a D collection with a D tonic is stated. That D tonic persists as stable even while the collections that include it change: we are brought through D, B♭, and G collections, all with D as the referential pitch until a burst of contrary motion chromaticism brings us back to an E♭ collection with an E♭ tonic that is slightly obscured and whose authority is somewhat challenged by the simultaneous arrival of an F in the bass.

This return to E♭, however transitory and attenuated, should give us time to pause and take stock of the larger tonal picture. Upon doing so we should see that the long tonal upbeat of the introduction has been followed by a stable region of E♭ tonic with E♭ collection which is in turn replaced by a series of collections with D as their tonic. The return to E♭ tonic and collection at rehearsal 11 should confirm that we are seeing a large-scale working out of the tonal relationships that we saw defined the tonic in their expression at the level of detail. (See ex. 11.) That is, the E♭ tonic was defined by a D–E♭ progression in the bass as part of the cadential resolution that characterized the introduction's move to the Allegro moderato, and this method of tonic definition is now composed out and reflected over the large scale of the composition by the larger scope of the tonal motion from an E♭ area to a D area back to an E♭ at rehearsal 11.

Starting at rehearsal 11 we see a reworking of the relationships already introduced. The material of rehearsal 11 is immediately sequenced down a step in a manner highly reminiscent of the sequential move at rehearsal 8. A third instance of the sequence is derailed and this is followed by an arrival on a D♭ collection with the second theme repeated, this time starting on A♭. Thus, something that had started to look much like a repetition of the tonal progressions of the beginning is redirected and we move in a completely different direction, one that does not circle back to E♭, but instead heads toward a strong octave D cadence that will close the exposition at rehearsal 14, a straightforward and obvious composing out of the

Example 11: Large-scale tonal motion.

Symbols used: Open note = local tonic: Filled note = secondary tone.

(A presumption of obligatory register is necessary.)

tonal relationships operative on the small scale. However clear that large-scale plan is, there are, nonetheless, a number of details that do not immediately reveal their role in this schema. Most obviously, a determination of the function of the collections used and the tonics established between rehearsal 11 and rehearsal 14 must be made if the large-scale picture is not to be viewed as arbitrary or selectively prescriptive.

Between the second theme area with its strongly defined D tonic and the close of the exposition with its striking multiple octave D cadence figure lies a restatement of the second theme starting on A♭ and an area where C is established as referential. An understanding of how these details fit into the larger tonal motion is dependent on following the surface voice leading and upon recalling the disposition of similar events in the introduction.

However, in order to understand those details we will need to backtrack a little to fit them into context. As mentioned, the return to E♭ at rehearsal 11 was weakened. The agent of that weakening was a strong F pedal in the lowest sounding voice (second bassoon). When the bass finally arrives on that E♭ two bars later it carries with it all of the voices in a sequential repetition that recalls similar events at rehearsal 8. A third instance of the sequence is deflected and instead the bass continues down to a C upon which it rests as a pedal over which the upper parts introduce the second theme, but this time starting on A♭, a tritone transposition from the original. This C pedal is the critical difference between this version of the second theme and the earlier statement at rehearsal 10. The C persists into the next section (rehearsal 13) and is not finally displaced as the bass note until the arrival of those powerful cadential octave D's at rehearsal 14. Furthermore, there is another crucial difference between the two statements of the second theme. The first time the melody skipped up from the D to a C♯ which then progressed on to a D, closing out the melodic figure in that instrument and rounding out the D octave in the process. However, in the restatement the comparable skip of A♭ to G is *not* continued up to A♭. Instead, the result is to have the A♭ resolve to the G. This is strongly supported by the doubling, particularly in the C trumpet, and the result is we can hear the resolution of the A♭ to a G over a C pedal. A summary of these observations shows that the section from rehearsal 11 to rehearsal 14 can best be construed as a neighbor expansion of the D tonic established earlier (ex. 12). Persuasive support for this view may be found in the introduction, where a prolonged C acted both as a neighbor to B♭ and as a passing tone from D to B♭ in the extended bass motion that projected the structural D–B♭ dyad that we saw served as the agent of tonal definition in the opening. Furthermore, the A♭–G resolution over the C that marks the end of the second theme's second statement was foreshadowed by similar surface events in the fifth bar of rehearsal 2 (ex. 13).

With the octave D's the exposition closes and with this figure the tonal procedures operative to this point achieve a definitive clarity: the same relationships we have seen as defining E♭ on the local level are worked out over a larger span as well. What is important to note in terms of hierarchy is that D, while established as a local tonic, is weakened in its independence and stability by the constantly shifting collectional grounds on which it stands. From that D tonic's first appearance it appears in four different collections: D, B♭, G, and C: four of the seven diatonic collections of which it could be a member. Because of this shifting ground we do not ascribe to that D tonic the referential stability that we have claimed for E♭ and this tends to support and confirm the many other details that express the E♭ as the referential tonic of the whole work with D as its principal supporter and definer.

The development section that now follows is notable for its complete lack of stable diatonic collections. Most of the collections are composed of linear chromatic segments or the coincidence of several diatonic collections partitioned among the instruments. This collectional profile prohibits any sense of closure and stability and it clearly distinguishes the interval content of this section from all of the other sections of the piece. This consistency of collectional use confirms the hypothesis suggested earlier about the function of different types of collections in the piece. However, more precision is necessary so that we might account for the specific patterns that appear in this section.

Example 12: Tonal motion from the second theme to the close of the exposition.

Bracketed notes indicate tonics whose function is weakened of deflected by strong secondary tones.

Example 13: Foreshadowing of C's function.

C functions as a "passing" degree between B♭ and D in the projection of that structural dyad and as a neighbor to B♭. Note the A♭–G support over that C. All these foreshadow similar treatment of C at rehearsal #13.

There is one constant feature that unifies the events of this section. With a good deal of regularity the various lines of the instruments throughout this development center around or gravitate toward D. Time and again they either start or end on D or have D support in the lowest voice. (See ex. 14.) Given the instability of the collectional base it would not be conceptually consistent to propose a D tonic for this section, but it is clear that D is in fact the anchor on and around which all of the melodic lines turn. Indeed, then, it seems as if Stravinsky has created an analogue to the prolongation of the dominant in tonal music. We have already seen how D functions as the definer of E♭ in the cadential motion from the introduction to the Allegro moderato and how that relationship was composed out as the large-scale framework for tonal motion in the exposition. Now the development section seems to act as an expansion of that role for D and thus builds the groundwork for a return to E♭, reflecting and expanding the meaning of harmonic motion that has been the underlying basis of tonal meaning in the piece to this point.

The expected return to E♭ comes five measures into rehearsal 17 and is stated with the repetition of that passage we had seen at rehearsal 11. As before, the return to E♭ is equivocally expressed. At rehearsal 18 the second theme returns, this time stated beginning on E. However, a second, altered statement occurs immediately, and this time the repetition is not at the tritone, but rather the first note of the

Example 14: Examples of D-oriented lines—development section. Igor Stravinsky, Octet for Winds. Copyright 1924 by Edition Russe de Musique; Renewed 1952. Copyright and renewal assigned to Boosey & Hawkes, Inc. Revised version copyright 1952 by Boosey & Hawkes, Inc. Renewed 1980. Reprinted by permission of Boosey & Hawkes, Inc.

theme, the referential note, is E♭. Instead of skipping a fifth as was done in all previous instances of this melody it skips only a fourth, from E♭ to A♭. However, we are not given an E♭ collection, but an incomplete and thus ambiguous diatonic collection. Following this is a series of passages formed of chromatic lines and partitioned diatonic collections that again defer tonic definition and stable collection, both of which features appear with the return of the Allegro moderato's first theme and a final arrival in a stable, though elaborated, eight-note diatonic collection.

What we see then is a kind of retrograde inversion recapitulation. Just as much as the exposition moved from an E♭-centered first theme to a D area for the second theme and then through an obscured E♭ to a closing cadence on D, so too here, by analogy, the recapitulation starts with that obscured E♭ tonic, moves inversionally backwards to an E second-theme area and closes with the rearrival on the E♭. (See ex. 15.)

The tonal procedures, initiated in the very first measures of the piece, have now come full circle and have found meaningful expression in a large-scale working out that supports or, more precisely, creates the formal structure of the composition. Stravinsky has not merely abstracted the superficial thematic pattern from classical sonata form and applied it uncritically to a new style. Rather, in a very real sense he has created a composition whose form expresses on the large scale those very ideas that were the nucleus of harmonic meaning on the surface. The familiar means of associating pitch and thematic repetition are used, not in an arbitrary gesture of homage to the past but in a constructive, coherent manner. Every detail of hierarchy (the type of collection, the level of transposition, the tonic assigned) functions as part of an interlocking system related to the formal design.

The logic and internal consistency of this structure testify to Stravinsky's mastery of the new idiom. They indicate the extent of his recognition of the critical problems of structural coherence, hierarchy, and stylistic consistency imposed on composers by the abandonment of traditional tonality. By coming to terms with these problems through the careful manipulation of his material, Stravinsky demonstrated a deep understanding of his musical past. He did not merely revere its external procedures but understood their inner meaning in such a way that he could create a new language based on familiar concepts. In so doing, he showed himself to be a composer who was capable of exploiting the past rather than one who was a slave to it.

Example 15: Summary of tonal motion.

54

CROSS-COLLECTIONAL TECHNIQUES OF STRUCTURE IN

Stravinsky's CENTRIC MUSIC

PAUL JOHNSON | *University of Notre Dame*

The stylistic diversity of Stravinsky's work may well be greater than that of any composer preceding him. Certainly it has attracted much attention. We are accustomed to the categorization of his works into disjunct periods (Russian, neoclassic, serial) and to an affirmation of the distinctive and differentiable character of each. That stylistic diversity has engendered a range of responses from celebration of Stravinsky's compositional virtuosity to disparagement of his music's alleged lack of a centered, easily classifiable focus.[1]

Yet many listeners believe that there *is* an underlying unity, so that beyond the spectacularly divergent forms, pitch materials, and harmonies there is an unmistakable, if elusive, "Stravinsky style." Given the genuine diversity of the surface of his music, such consistency could only be found in common underlying procedures and techniques. I contend that significant similarities exist in the techniques Stravinsky used to articulate the properties of two favored collections: the octatonic and 0123578t collections. I further assert that these similarities may well lie at the root of that ephemeral consistency which seems to cut across Stravinsky's first two compositional periods. To provide a proper framework in support of these claims, I will first discuss some properties of the two collections, then examine their similarities (and differences), and finally show how Stravinsky exploits and manipulates them in ways that indicate shared stylistic procedures.

0123578t, hereafter known as the eight-note diatonic collection, appears in many of Stravinsky's works from 1918 to 1951.[2] This collection can be derived in several ways. (Rather than examine all the possibilities I will discuss only those that possess properties exploited by Stravinsky.) Unordered, it can be considered the union of any two diatonic collections that share six pitch classes. Stravinsky seems to favor a limited range of the possible derivations. (1) By generating the collection

1. See Paul Henry Lang, introduction in *Stravinsky: A New Appraisal of His Work,* ed. Paul Henry Lang (New York: Norton, 1963), pp. 9–19.

2. The appendix to this paper lists places in Stravinsky's compositions where the collection can be found. A further exposition of properties of the collection can be found in my dissertation "The First Movement of Stravinsky's *Symphony in C*: Its Syntactical Bases and Their Implications" (especially pp. 25–34), Ph. D dissertation, Princeton University 1981 (University Microfilms, Ann Arbor).

3. In the Violin Concerto it is significant that the D–E–A sonority (the "passport to the concerto") that opens each movement can be generated in perfect fifths since the large-scale polarity of the first movement of the concerto is a perfect fifth, reflecting the opening harmony in the same way that 047e reflects major-third polarity.

4. See Arthur Berger, "Problems of Pitch Organization in Stravinsky," *Perspectives of New Music* 2, no. 2 (1963), and Pieter van den Toorn, "Some Characteristics of Stravinsky's Diatonic Music," *Perspectives of New Music* 14, no. 1 (Fall-Winter 1975):104–38; 15, no. 2 (Spring-Summer 1977):58–95.

5. Stravinsky seemed to be attracted to this class of collection even in his serial period. See the transpositionally symmetrical "rows" at the beginning of the Gigue of the Septet.

from two diatonic collections a fifth apart, each ordered 024579e (the major scale), two possible referential orderings are feasible, depending on which of the two origins is emphasized. For example, if the collection is generated from the C- and G-major scales, then a referential center on C creates an ordering of 0245679e (hereafter referred to as the ♯4 ordering). If G is assigned referential priority, then the ordering is 024579te (hereafter referred to as the ♭7 ordering) (ex. 1). (2) If the referential collection is generated from a diatonic scale (ordered 024579e, the major scale) and another diatonic scale (ordered 023578t, the natural minor scale) a major third higher, then again two potential orderings result. If the C-major scale is combined with the E natural minor collection and C is assigned referential priority, then again the ♯4 ordering results: 0245679e. If E is considered the referential cr the ordering 0123578t (the ♭2 ordering) results (ex. 2).

Since major-third relationships seem to predominate in Stravinsky's works that use this collection, it is significant that the referential sonority characteristic of works using the eight-note diatonic collection reflects those very intervallic relationships. In these pieces the referential sonority, (the "tonic") is often a 047e tetrachord. Thus the 047e built on C (CEGB) contains both the C-major and E-minor triads (and only those triads) thus delineating a polarity between triads a major third apart.[3]

Since the octatonic collection has been discussed at length elsewhere, it does not require extensive discussion here.[4] Rather, we can turn directly to an examination of the similarities and differences between it and the eight-note diatonic collection. This will offer a firm basis for examining the shared techniques Stravinsky employs to articulate construct dependent centers.

We can begin by noting that the two collections are both members of the class of eight-note symmetrical collections.[5] The symmetry of both collections creates the potential for an ambiguous hierarchy of tones. In the eight-note diatonic collection, CDEFF♯GAB, F♯ divides the C octave symmetrically, but by the same criterion, C may symmetrically divide the F♯ octave. Stravinsky does not explicitly

Example 1

C(♯4) - 0 2 4 5 6 7 9 e   G(♭7) - 0 2 4 5 7 9 t e

Example 2

C(♯4)   E(♭2) - 0 1 2 3 5 7 8 t

Example 3

exploit this tritone symmetry, but uses F♯ to create content differentiation between the two diatonic collections present in the collection. Thus this collection (unlike its diatonic antecedent) has two areas of polarity, created by the symmetry, and bound up with such polarity is the potential for change of referential center without change of collection. By contrast, the octatonic collection divides the octave symmetrically in two ways: at the tritone and at a further subdivision into minor thirds (ex. 3). This can provide four areas of polarity each of which also retains the original collection and referential ordering.

Some interesting similarities and important differences between the collections emerge in a comparison of the possible interactions between assigned tonic and referential ordering. The similarities lie in Stravinsky's common practice of extracting different tonics from the same collection or, conversely, extracting the same tonic from different collections. The differences are created by particular properties of the two collections. In the octatonic there are eight possible tonics but only two referential orderings; in the eight-note diatonic collection, there are three preferred tonics, but each establishes a unique ordering. Given an assigned tonic in the octatonic collection, there are only two distinct collections that could embrace such a fixed center and these two collections have different orderings; an assigned tonic in the eight-note system is a member of three different collections, each with a different referential ordering. Examining the interaction of collection and referential ordering shows the following. In the octatonic collection there is a relatively limited number of interactions: there are only three distinct collections and two possible referential orderings. With the eight-note diatonic collection there is a wide range of possibilities: twelve distinct collections and three preferred orderings. In the eight-note diatonic collection, this permits different tonics to embrace the same collection, but with different referential orderings (e.g., *CDEFF♯GAB* = 0245679e, or *EFF♯GABCD* = 0123578t, or *GABCDEFF♯* = 024579te) creating thirty-six possible "areas" within the system (i.e., twelve possible tonics times three referential orderings). In the octatonic system this is also possible, but in a more limited manner. That is, if the tonics are related by T3, T6, or T9, the collection and referential ordering remain fixed. But if the tonics are related by the remaining transpositions, then either the ordering or the collection is altered. This creates twenty-four possible "areas" within the system (twelve possible tonics times two referential orderings).

6. For further views of an idea of a nontriadic referential sonority, see Roy Travis, "Towards a New Concept of Tonality?," *Journal of Music Theory* 3, no. 2 (November 1959):257–84, and Johnson, "The First Movement of Stravinsky's *Symphony in C.*"

There are similarities not only between the collections themselves but also between some of the significant sonorities extracted from each. In ♯4 ordering of the eight-note diatonic collection Stravinsky uses the 047e and 037t tetrachords as normative harmonic sonorities, perhaps analogous to the triad in the tonal system.[6] In the octatonic system, the 0347 tetrachord seems to have a similar if less systematic function. These three tetrachords, 047e, 037t, and 0347 are three of the seven tetrachords that are (1) symmetrical and (2) have two duplicated intervals and two unique intervals (ex. 4). The three tetrachords used by Stravinsky are the only ones containing triads, and in which the intervals of the triad (major third, minor third, perfect fifth) provide the duplicated intervals of these tetrachords (ex. 5). These three tetrachords (and only these three) can be generated when any given interval of a triad (P5, M3, m3) is transposed by either of the remaining two.

The intervallic formation of these tetrachords, two duplicated intervals and two unique intervals, is precisely suited to the polarities that Stravinsky frequently employs. The duplicated major thirds of the 0347 tetrachord provide two disjunct but equal intervals that are related by transposition at the minor third, one of the structural intervals of the octatonic collection. Similarly, one of the sets of duplicated intervals in the 047e (P5s) is related by transposition by a major third, reflecting the major-third polarity inherent in Stravinsky's ordering of the eight-note diatonic collection. This similarity of generative structure between 047e and 0347 affords analogous invariances under transposition in the octatonic system. For example, the polarity of C and A, expressed via 0347 built on those tones, will retain as common tones C and E, one of the duplicated major thirds (ex. 6). The intervallic relation inherent in the symmetrical tetrachord provides for an extension of minor-third interaction to a polarity between any minor-third-related tetrachord.

Example 4

0347   047e   037t   0134   0145   0235   0156

Example 5

037t   0347   047e

Example 6

The duple symmetry of both tetrachords is necessary to the system, for with groupings of two identical musical units, say two transpositionally related tetrachords, there is equality in terms of their relations to one another, and therefore ambiguity (or polarity) is likely. However, with a group of three equivalent units (excepting those related by 048), a given unit cannot possess the same relations to the remaining units as they have to each other. In the 0347 and 047e tetrachords, Stravinsky has used the two intervals of equal size that, because of their duple symmetry, provide opportunities both for construct centric composing and for polarized local centers.

A further relation between the collections and tetrachords concerns the intervallic multiplicity of the collections. The eight-note diatonic collection (like the diatonic collection) can be generated by the cycle of fifths. The perfect fifth is not only the generator of this collection, and thus its interval of greatest multiplicity, but is also one of the duplicated intervals in the 047e tetrachord, the referential tonic like sonority in pieces using that collection.

The 0347 tetrachord is related to the octatonic collection in a strikingly similar manner. The interval of greatest multiplicity in the octatonic collection is the minor third and is essential in any generation scheme for this collection.[7] In this sense we can regard the minor third (in the octatonic collection) as structurally similar to the perfect fifth in the eight-note diatonic system. Therefore the 0347 tetrachord holds a similar structural function in relation to the octatonic collection as the 047e does with respect to the eight-note diatonic collection. In both cases a structural interval of the collection (P5 and m3 respectively) are related by the other duplicated interval of the respective tetrachord (major third in both cases) (ex. 7).

A further shared property is that the two tetrachords generate their respective collections under transposition since each tetrachord omits an interval class of the collection. The 047e tetrachord transposed a major second generates the eight-note diatonic collection; the 0347 tetrachord transposed a tritone generates the octatonic collection.

The similarities between the two collections, the structural correspondences of their tetrachords, and the similar function of these tetrachords in their respective collections provide us with interesting and provocative theoretical bases from which we may undertake a search for the underlying if ephemeral compositional unity that cuts across the oft-cited and obvious stylistic divisions. It is my conten-

7. The tritone is of the same multiplicity as the minor third if you count each tritone twice (e.g., B–F, F–B).

Example 7

tion that the significant cross-collectional correspondences discussed above are articulated by parallel techniques from style to style. Clearly, given the relations between the two collections, such identical techniques used to articulate the polarities of the collections must necessarily display more than casual functional similitude and the degree of intersection of function will be determined by the similarity of the collections, not merely by the identity of the operations.[8]

8. Inversion is a familiar example of an operation that changes function when applied in two different systems. When used in a twelve-tone piece its function as a basic operation of the system is very different from an inversion in a tonal composition, where it is generally a means of melodic transformation and not basic to the system. The operation can be identical from system to system, but the context of the operation changes its function. Thus the identical techniques used in octatonic and eight-note diatonic compositions will only be functionally similar to the extent that the collections are related.

To support these theoretical suppositions I will now cite concrete musical examples and show how individual techniques articulate the two collections. I will draw my octatonic examples primarily from *Zvezdoliki,* a secular cantata of 1912. The eight-note diatonic examples will come from a variety of pieces. In both cases these examples must be understood as representative of the repertoires of which they are a part.

Our first such shared technique is that of diatonic articulation. This technique may be described as the use of diatonic elements (with their historically dependent stability) to articulate one element of a construct centric area.

The first movement of the Symphony in C is polarized between C and E centers. At a crucial point in the movement (the exact center) the primary theme, heretofore stated in C, is reinterpreted in E. Stravinsky extracts the E-minor collection from the movement's referential eight-note diatonic collection (ex. 8). The absence of F♮ provides the movement with a large-scale, thematically defined articulation of the basic polarity of the movement. Thus E minor, with its opportunities for a stable E hierarchy, helps to articulate the basic polarity of the movement.

Example 8: Igor Stravinsky, Symphony in C. Copyright Schott & Co., Ltd., London, 1948. Copyright renewed 1976. All rights reserved. Used by permission of European American Music Distributors Corporation, sole U.S. agent for Schott & Co., Ltd.

On the small scale, the opening of *Zvezdoliki* employs a similar technique of articulation (ex. 9). Although the primary referential center of the piece is C, Stravinsky establishes the basic intervallic polarity of the work, the minor third, from the very beginning. The opening three chords move from an 0347 tetrachord with C in the bass to an 0247 tetrachord (with A in the bass) that is not present in the octatonic collection defined by the first two chords (nor any octatonic collection) but is rather a segment of the A-major collection (an A-major triad with an added ninth). The disposition of the chords supports the diatonic articulation of this fundamental minor third, C–A, relationship. The A–B–D♭–E tetrachord has the ambit of a perfect fifth, with A–E doubled, as does the C–E♭–E–G tetrachord that has C–G doubled, thus providing a weighted C–G to A–E motion spanning a minor third.

The implicit polarity of the collections and their tetrachords provides the materials for such polarities. However, the isolation of the polarity-producing harmonies within a composition is necessary to create the harmonic systems that I have been describing. Partitioning of the referential sonorities, by register or by instrumentation, provides one means through which Stravinsky can create the polarities inherent in his two pitch systems.

As noted, symmetrical partitioning of 047e or 0347 can express a polarity that

Example 9: Igor Stravinsky, Zvezdoliki. Copyright 1971 renewed by Rob. Forberg–P. Jurgenson. Reprinted by permission of C. F. Peters Corporation, sole selling agents for Rob. Forberg.

Paul Johnson

Ex. 9 (cont.)

is supported by the collection from which it is derived. For example, partitioning the 047e tetrachord into perfect fifths, C–G, E–B, expresses a C–E polarity, whereas C–E, G–B is considered a symmetrical tetrachord based on C, stacked in thirds or a polarity between C and G. The two unique intervals of 047e, the major seventh and the minor third, have entirely different functions. The major seventh can define the tetrachord as being C-based, since E minor's function in the 047e would be subsumed by its outside interval. The minor third of 047e provides an ambiguity since it is the shared interval of the C-major and E-minor triads.

The opening of the first theme of the Symphony in C illustrates the functions of these intervals (ex. 10). The dyad B–C in the oboe represents the unique half-step in the C–E–G–B tetrachord. Stated above the E–G pedal in the strings, the polarity of C major and E minor is expressed both in that the E–G third is common

62

to both triads, and that the B–C motion presents both triads within the context of the referential 047e tetrachord.

A similar kind of partitioning of the 0347 tetrachord is present in *Zvezdoliki,* with similar results for the articulation of centricity within the octatonic system (ex. 9).

In the opening 0347 tetrachord of *Zvezdoliki,* the doubled pitches, C–G (a unique interval of the tetrachord), and the placement of C in the bass encourage a view of this 0347 as a unit based on C. At the same time, the outer intervals, E♭–G and C–E, implicate the subsequently exploited polarity of areas a minor third apart. Thus the perfect fifth in the 0347, its outside interval, can be construed to have the same function as the major seventh in 047e: both help articulate their tetrachords as units. On the other hand, the symmetrical partition of 0347 into major thirds and 047e into perfect fifths encourages the expression of an underlying polarity.

A motivic reworking of the top voice of the vocal chords immediately follows these opening chords. In the reworking, E♭ replaces E and subsequently moves back to E at number 1. That E is part of a C-based tetrachord in which E♭ has been replaced by F♯, the ♯4. Both tetrachords are part of the same octatonic collection.

The tetrachord C–E–F♯–G (hereafter called the all-interval tetrachord) is partitioned so that E–C is assigned to the voice parts while E–F♯–G appears in the orchestra.[9] While the orchestral notes are held as pedals, the next chord is an 0347 tetrachord on A, relating by a minor third to the 0347 on C of the opening and thus to the C–A motion of the opening harmonies in the choir. This minor-third motion supports the function of the symmetrical partition of the 0347 on C (C–E, E♭–G) and the C–E vocal partition from the C all-interval tetrachord. C–E then becomes part of the major-third symmetrical partition of 0347 on A. A return to an all-interval tetrachord on C is followed by an all-interval tetrachord on A (another minor-third connection). This latter tetrachord retains E♭–E from the 0347 on C. The half-step of 0347 tetrachord (its middle interval) provides two common tones between an 0347 tetrachord and the all-interval tetrachord a minor third below. This is then roughly analogous to the function of the minor third in 047e (its middle interval), which is the shared interval of the two polarity-defining triads of the tetrachord.

Continuing with an examination of *Zvezdoliki's* chords and their partitionings until the phrase end in measure 7, one can see that the final vocal partition of 0347 on C is in major thirds, E♭–G, and C–E (spaced as a minor sixth), reflecting the minor-third polarities that are composed out in measures 3–6. Minor-third emphases are seen most obviously in measures 6–7. In the orchestra in measures 6–7 an E♭

9. This designation is merely for convenience and not to imply any special status for its all-interval properties. Nor does it imply that 0146 (the other all-interval tetrachord) will be of use in the system.

triad moves to C major, fulfilling the implications of the opening partitioning and preparing the vocal and orchestral cadence on C in the second half of measure 7. The vocal music of measures 6–7 can be seen as an elaboration of this basic motion. The vocal pitches accompanying the E♭-major triad begin with an all-interval tetrachord on A which, when combined with the E♭ triad, adds up to an E♭ triad extended in thirds. The orchestrational partition of the two sonorities defines another chordal relationship by structural interval, the tritone. The final two vocal sonorities of the bar, D♭ with an added ninth and B♭-minor seventh, lead by minor-third sequence to a G-major ninth without a third which extends by thirds the C-major triad of the orchestra. Within the context of a bass linearization of 0347 on C (G–C–D♯–E), a similar minor third chord sequence in the vocal parts leads to C: F♯ all-interval tetrachord to A all-interval tetrachord to 0347 on C. In the last motion there is a voice exchange between second tenor and bass (E–E♭ and D♯–E) that linearizes the half-step of the 0347 tetrachord and illustrates its function as the shared interval of the 0347 tetrachord and the all-interval tetrachord a minor third below.

The final chord of the phrase can be reasonably partitioned on the basis of register and orchestration into the C 0347 and C all-interval tetrachords.

This kind of partitioning of relatable units on registral, orchestrational, or rhythmic grounds can now be seen at a number of levels:

1. The partitioning of the normative sonority into its duplicated intervals to suggest the basic polarity of the work.

2. A temporal diminution in which one element of the partition is moving in the basic intervallic structure while another defined element is elaborating that intervallic motion—in *Zvezdoliki*, E♭–C motion in the orchestra while D♭–B♭–G and F♯–A–C motions elaborate the basic minor-third relation in the chorus.

3. The partitioning of a large chord so that it may be understood as a conjunction of two different normative sonorities (the C 0347 and C all-interval tetrachords in measure 7).

The registral partitioning of relatable units is an extremely common technique in eight-note diatonic music also. The Rondoletto of the Serenade in A is a good example (ex. 11). The arpeggiation of C♯-minor triads (with B-minor passing chords) are registrally juxtaposed against the slower unfolding of the A-major triad in the right hand. The C♯-minor and A-major triads together form the normative

Example 11: Igor Stravinsky,
Serenade en la. Copyright
1926 by Edition Russe de
Musique; Renewed 1958.
Copyright assigned 1947 to
Boosey and Hawkes, Inc.
Reprinted by permission of
Boosey & Hawkes, Inc.

10. One can also see a similar
kind of partitioning at the
opening of the second part of
The Rite of Spring. The hexachord 013478 is registrally
partitioned into the D-minor
triad with E♭ minor alternating with C♯ minor (both
form the same hexachord
when combined with D
minor). This partitioning also
recalls the famous chord from
the *Dance of the Adolescents*.

11. Berger, p. 16.

harmony 047e of the eight-note diatonic collection, in this case built on A, and express the basic polarity of the collection through registral partitioning.[10]

Stravinsky employed a number of other shared techniques to articulate the fundamental properties of his collections. These techniques include registral, ca-dential, and harmonic formulaic articulation and occur in remarkably similar ways in the different collections. A brief survey should be sufficient to indicate the extent to which these techniques contribute to the underlying cross-collectional unity.

A common registral technique used by Stravinsky is the placing into the bass of a note he wishes to articulate as the referential tone of an ambiguous harmonic structure, or conversely, placing a tone in the bass to color an unambiguous struc-ture. By isolating a tone in the lower register, repeating it, and orchestrationally doubling it for emphasis, Stravinsky has a simple, though effective, technique that is common not only to octatonic and eight-note diatonic works but to diatonic works as well.[11]

A cadential sonority in the orchestra at rehearsal 3 of *Zvezdoliki* supplies a good example of this technique (ex. 12). This sonority cannot be understood in terms of any of the referential sonorities of the work (0347, all-interval tetrachord) but can be understood as articulative of A simply because A is the bass tone and no other suitable candidate for root of the sonority can be found. One advantage of under-standing A as the root of the chord is that the chord that precedes this harmony (not shown) can be understood as having C as its root.

The final chord of the Symphony in C provides an example from an eight-note diatonic piece (ex. 13). That sonority (C–E–G–B) is heard most often in the work as an 047e based on C. However, at the close of the movement the strong

65

Ex. 12

Ex. 13

Example 12: Igor Stravinsky, Zvezdoliki. Copyright 1971 renewed by Rob. Forberg–P. Jurgenson. Reprinted by permission of C. F. Peters Corporation, sole selling agents for Rob. Forberg.

Example 13: Igor Stravinsky, Symphony in C. Copyright Schott & Co., Ltd., London, 1948. Copyright renewed 1976. All rights reserved. Used by permission of European American Music Distributors Corporation, sole U.S. agent for Schott & Co., Ltd.

emphasis on E in the bass (alongside some other formal and voice-leading emphases) creates a cadence on E minor with an added sixth.

Another shared technique is found in the way phrase endings ("cadences") are used to articulate referential points. In the absence of common practice syntax (where such phrases are delineated by melodic and harmonic procedures) Stravinsky uses the temporal emphasis placed on the outer points of a phrase to

66

highlight a referential norm by isolating it from its surroundings. (This procedure is akin to the articulative status assigned to the end of a sequence in tonal music.) Examples can be found throughout the literature.

The first three chords of *Zvezdoliki*, isolated temporally and orchestrationally from what follows, provide a good example of a minor-third delineation. In eight-note diatonic compositions opening ideas that establish a referential norm are frequently isolated by silence, orchestration, or register. One need only examine the opening ideas of compositions such as *Apollo*, Serenade in A, Violin Concerto, or *Jeu de cartes* to see how registral, temporal, and orchestrational isolation is used.[12]

Finally, certain contextually established harmonic formulas may be used to articulate the underlying structure. At rehearsal 9 in *Zvezdoliki* a series of articulations of minor-third-related motions proceed to a final goal on G which is given registral and diatonic emphasis (ex. 14). Such local harmonic logic is used in similar ways in eight-note diatonic pieces. Since tonic-dominant relations are not an *a priori* harmonic relation in this repertoire, Stravinsky establishes this harmonic connection at the opening of the Symphony in C (ex. 15). Having established the progression contextually, and having isolated it orchestrationally, Stravinsky is then free to use the progression syntactically. Immediately preceding the first theme of the first movement Stravinsky generates a good deal of harmonic tension by prolonging the dominant and then resolving it to tonic at the first theme (ex. 16). Because the progression has been established as part of the language of the piece, it no longer needs to be isolated to be understood as a harmonic connection.

12. For a somewhat different view of the compositional motivation for the isolation of gestures in Stravinsky's music, see Edward T. Cone, "Stravinsky: The Progress of a Method," in *Perspectives on Schoenberg and Stravinsky*, ed. Benjamin Boretz and Edward T. Cone (Princeton, N.J.: Princeton University Press, 1968), pp. 156–64.

Example 14: Igor Stravinsky, Zvezdoliki. Copyright 1971 renewed by Rob. Forberg–P. Jurgenson. Reprinted by permission of C. F. Peters Corporation, sole selling agents for Rob. Forberg.

Example 15: Igor Stravinsky, Symphony in C. Copyright Schott & Co., Ltd., London, 1948. Copyright renewed 1976. All rights reserved. Used by permission of European American Music Distributors Corporation, sole U.S. agent for Schott & Co., Ltd.

Most of the shared techniques discussed so far exert their influence on local continuities, articulations, and progressions. As a final area of cross-collectional correspondence, I would like to turn my attention to longer spans of musical time. Stravinsky employs similar techniques of articulation of the referential sonorities of the two collections through time. The tonal motion of the compositions can best

be understood in the context of Schenkerian concepts of linear unfolding of a harmony, the 0347 tetrachord in the octatonic compositions, 047e in the eight-note diatonic works.

Measures 9–10 of *Zvezdoliki*, a transitional passage, provide one example of minor-third linear unfoldings that compose out the basic structural interval of the work (ex. 17). The upper parts show parallel perfect fifth unfoldings C–E♭ and F–A♭, E♭–F♯ and A♭–B while the bass unfolds B♭–D♭, D♭–E, and E–G. It is important to note that the unfoldings here fall into two categories: those that are specifically polarity-defining and those that are simply motivic.

69

A passage at rehearsal 8 unfolds an E♭–C relationship and shows E♭ to be part of a composing-out of a basic unfolding of the 0347 tetrachord on C (ex. 18). In a sense, a chordal motion E♭–C may be considered as a linearization of this tetrachord.

The passage in example 18 cadences on a diatonically articulative C-major ninth chord. Two statements of a minor-third transposition of the opening melody show that the opening tune holds one common tone, G, between the 0347 tetrachords a minor third apart. In the upper voice unfolding, B♭ moves to C (D♭♭) placing E♭ 0347 within the span of the C 0347 prolongation.

In the bass, E♭, a common tone of the 0347 tetrachords on C and E♭ and root of the E♭ 0347 tetrachord at the beginning of the bar, is shown in the bass unfolding to be part of a linearization of the 0347 on C. The vocal parts for the most part merely arpeggiate a C 0347 (bass voice, second tenor) or emphasize C in a motion with a motivic function. The first tenor inflects C with motivic A–C motion, and the baritone uses an F♯ neighbor to G in a C–G arpeggiation that recalls the all-interval tetrachord on C.

Similar linear techniques can be found in eight-note diatonic works. The similar contour and function of the opening motive of the Symphony in C, B–C–G, is much like the common tone functions of example 18 (ex. 19). In that motive, C and G are root and fifth of C major, G and B are third and fifth of E minor, the two triads that express the basic polarity of the first movement. In the opening of

Example 18: Igor Stravinsky, *Zvezdoliki*. Copyright 1971 renewed by Rob. Forberg–P. Jurgenson. Reprinted by permission of C. F. Peters Corporation, sole selling agents for Rob. Forberg.

Zvezdoliki, A and E are root and fifth of A major while E and G are third and fifth of C major, the minor-third polarity of the work. The opening second of both motives is the interval that cannot be part of the polarity-defining intervals or triads. The opening of *Apollo* and the opening duet of *The Rake's Progress* show similar functional melodic formations.

In a larger frame, example 20 provides a reduction of eleven bars of the introduction of the Symphony in C that prolongs the 047e on C linearly, and expresses the C–E polarity registrally. In the outer voices there is an unfolding G–C with an octave transferred A–B in the upper part. In the bass, the graph shows an octave unfolding E–E with a bass arpeggiation of the E-minor triad. The two unfoldings together create C 047e. The registral delineation of the C-major and E-minor triads is clearly related to the registral partitioning techniques discussed in relation to the Serenade in A and *Zvezdoliki*.

The shared techniques that have been described suggest a way of understanding Stravinsky's music that emphasizes a continuity of practice that cuts across the

Example 19:

71

Paul Johnson

Example 20: Igor Stravinsky, Symphony in C. Copyright Schott & Co., Ltd., London, 1948. Copyright renewed 1976. All rights reserved. Used by permission of European American Music Distributors Corporation, sole U.S. agent for Schott & Co., Ltd.

Ex. 20 (cont.)

Ex. 20 (cont.)

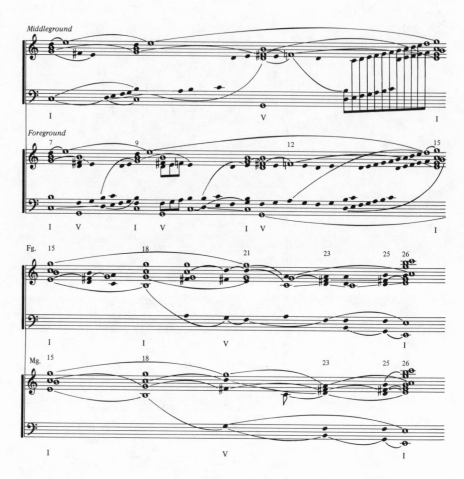

prominent stylistic divisions. Let me close by citing two remarks of the composer that tend to support this view of his work.

I have always composed with intervals.

What preoccupies us, then, is less tonality, properly so called, then what might be described as the polarity of a sound, of an interval, or even of a sonic complex.[13]

13. Igor Stravinsky, *Poetique Musicale* (Cambridge Mass.: Harvard University Press, 1942), p. 26.

I think that these remarks support the theoretical concepts advanced above. Not only are the latent polarities of a collection and the tetrachord ("sonic complex") derived from the collection used as the basic background from which Stravinsky worked, but these properties are derived from the symmetrical intervallic properties of both the collections. Indeed, this theory shows that in regard to the octatonic and eight-note diatonic relations, it is the intervals that are the basic material, not the tetrachords. These intervals are delineated registrally, orchestrationally, temporally, linearly, harmonically, rhythmically, in virtually all the familiar compositional domains. Moreover, these basic relations are used at all levels of structure, providing coherent pitch languages that are articulated via a common body of techniques that function in extremely related ways to express basic intervallic relations of the collections.

APPENDIX

Piece	*Place*	*Ordering*
Histoire du soldat	Great Chorale	G ($\flat\hat{7}$)
Octet	Rehearsal 7	E$\flat$ ($\flat\hat{7}$)
Concerto for Piano	opening of II	C ($\sharp\hat{4}$)
Serenade in A	opening of I	F ($\sharp\hat{4}$)
	Romanza 3/8	G ($\sharp\hat{4}$)
	Rondoletto	A ($\flat\hat{7}$)
Apollo	opening	C ($\sharp\hat{4}$)
Le baiser de la fée	Rehearsal 14–15	F ($\flat\hat{7}$)
Capriccio	” 54	G ($\flat\hat{7}$)
Violin Concerto	” 1	D ($\flat\hat{7}$)
Perséphone	” 153–154	C ($\sharp\hat{4}$)
Jeu de cartes	opening	B$\flat$ ($\sharp\hat{4}$)
"Dumbarton Oaks" Concerto	Rehearsal 88–end	E$\flat$ ($\flat\hat{7}$)
Symphony in C	I	C ($\sharp\hat{4}$)
Danses concertantes	opening	B$\flat$ ($\flat\hat{7}$)
Sonata for Two Pianos	opening	F ($\sharp\hat{4}$)
Elegy	Lento	G ($\flat\hat{2}$)
Symphony in Three Movements	opening of II	D ($\sharp\hat{4}$) with a $\flat$3
Orpheus	Rehearsal 101	F ($\sharp\hat{4}$), F ($\flat\hat{7}$)
Mass	Gloria	A mixolydian ($\sharp\hat{7}$)
The Rake's Progress	Introduction	E ($\sharp\hat{4}$) ($\flat\hat{7}$)
Cantata	Lyke-Wake Dirge	
	versus 2	C ($\sharp\hat{4}$)
Greeting Prelude		C ($\sharp\hat{4}$)
Canticum sacrum	Dedicatio	G ($\flat\hat{7}$)
Agon	opening	C ($\sharp\hat{4}$)

CONUNDRUMS, CONJECTURES, CONSTRUALS; OR 5 VS. 3:

THE INFLUENCE OF RUSSIAN COMPOSERS ON *Stravinsky*

CLAUDIO SPIES | *Princeton University*

By way of explaining the unequal contest suggested by the alternate heading, it may be helpful to reduce the first numeral, referring to the *maguchia kuchka* or "mighty heap," as it was known, to its single apposite representative in Stravinsky's lifetime: his teacher Rimsky-Korsakov. (Of the other four *kuchkisti,* only Mussorgsky's music meant anything to Stravinsky: he professed great admiration for its originality and as heartily detested Rimsky's bowdlerizing compositional corrections and substitutions, particularly in *Boris Godunov.*) As for the second numeral, that might likewise be reduced to one—in this case, Tchaikovsky—but little purpose would be served simply by eliminating the other two composers on that side, Glinka and Dargomyzhsky, inasmuch as the music of each of the three held a very particular place among Stravinsky's early impressions. A sweeping reduction of contenders to one on either side, though neat, and quite accurately descriptive of fiercely antagonistic feelings that endured well beyond Stravinsky's twentieth year—even though Tchaikovsky had been dead and buried for the last fifteen years of Rimsky's life—would nonetheless be insensitive to several of the questions at hand.

As the son of a leading bass at the Saint Petersburg Opera, and living less than a city block from the Maryinsky Theater, Stravinsky as a child must have seen his father in a good many Russian operas, including both of Glinka's, two of Dargomyzhsky's, and probably several of Tchaikovsky's, as well as such new productions as Rimsky-Korsakov's *Mlada, Christmas Eve,* and *Sadko.* (It is unlikely, however, that Stravinsky would at the age of five have been taken to see his father first sing the evil monk Mamyirov in Tchaikovsky's *Sorceress,* but he did see *The Sleeping Beauty* during its first season, in 1890.) We know that during his adolescence and later Stravinsky attended not only performances but had free access to virtually all opera rehearsals at the Maryinsky, at which he often sat next to Rimsky-

76

Korsakov and through which he became acquainted with many of the performers taking part. We may therefore reasonably conclude that a very large part of the Russian music Stravinsky heard before the age of twenty-five was operatic, and that his subsequent prevailing association with the musical stage—through either ballet or opera or mixtures of both—must have had its roots mainly in those early experiences. Since such a conclusion is neither difficult to draw nor to substantiate, what, then, are the conundrums, conjectures, and construals of this paper's heading? In answering that question, we should first deal with a few preliminaries by means of which we may define, and find contexts for, these conundrums, conjectures, and construals.

They have to do, specifically, with documentary evidence that remains inaccessible either through loss or concealment or failure of discovery. (The material I am thinking of has been in Russia, and may still be there, waiting to be dug up; or else it has been kept under wraps by officialdom for reasons none of us could fathom; or else it has really been destroyed or lost.) But there are also more generic reasons governing the choice of these alliterative words, and they are difficult to pinpoint because a mere mention of them is apt to be misleading, and even the briefest plunge into their murky shallows may easily be misunderstood. The vagaries of Russian music history are such that it is very tempting to interpret it only in terms of the primary sharp contrast between itself and Western European music history: whereas nineteenth-century Western European music was based upon a largely shared tradition of compositional practice and theory, in Russia that tradition was to a great extent lacking, or was, at least, rooted outside Russian territory. The degree to which this apparently simplistic view might nonetheless be tenable is worth examining briefly in light of Stravinsky's work both prior and subsequent to his first successes in Paris.

It should not be necessary, at this point, to dwell on the fact that, for most Russian composers in the nineteenth century, composing was not so much a professional activity as either a "gentleman's avocation" or, at any rate, something other than one's principal line of work. All of the composers mentioned so far had initially been prepared for professions that had no connection whatever with music—a circumstance not unfamiliar, after all, to numerous Western European composers—but in addition to that, the kind of musical training each of these men had received could range from the trivially useless to the pertinent and productive. Certainly, both Glinka and Tchaikovsky stand out as uniquely aware of the professional nature of their abilities and endeavors: Tchaikovsky the more so, by virtue of his having been both the first Russian composer trained entirely in a Russian music school, and one whose career involved extensive professional activity abroad;

Glinka increasingly so, in view of his painstaking studies of counterpoint, at various times and even late in life, with the theorist Siegfried Dehn in Berlin, as well as through his encounters and musical associations with John Field, Bellini, Donizetti, and Berlioz. In any case, it is to these two composers that we can turn for accessible and obvious clues as to the mix of Western European compositional skills and a predilection for—for whatever reason—"Russian" musical materials that was ultimately to mean so much to Stravinsky's own relation to Russian music. If we consider the other composers named at the outset—Dargomyzhsky and the *kuchkisti*—in this context, we must distinguish between the two who assumed leading positions by repeatedly proving their willingness to "correct" or "improve upon" the work of their colleagues, and these same colleagues who either agreed to collaborative efforts or who had died by the time such clean-up jobs were undertaken. The two are Rimsky, who orchestrated, and probably fiddled with, Dargomyzhsky's opera *The Stone Guest*—César Cui added some music at Dargomyzhsky's dying request—and Balakirev, who added two entr'actes to Glinka's *Ruslan and Lyudmila*. What these men particularly shared was a stringent— sometimes even strident—cultivation of their music's "Russianness," more often than not at the expense of compositional refinements practiced elsewhere in Europe at the time. They also made common cause of their disdain for Italian operatic usage, a position thanks to which they collided headlong and permanently with Tchaikovsky's and Glinka's devotion to that model. What this meant, in slightly more specific terms, with regard to Glinka and Tchaikovsky, is that whereas Glinka emulated bel canto vocal writing, often highly ornamented with *fioriture* and cadenzas, no matter how "Russian" a particular aria might sound—Tchaikovsky's vocal habits were somewhat less flamboyant—on their own terms they each worked successfully toward maintaining functional distinctions between vocal lines and orchestral accompaniments, toward achieving the greatest variety and elegance of detail in their instrumental writing, and above all, toward assembling continuities whose textural, rhythmic, harmonic, tempo-related, and accentual timing is as precise and concise as the dramatic action and the text at hand might call for. (If this last operatic phenomenon is not necessarily a by-product only of Italian models, it is nevertheless usually to be ascertained without any trouble in what I make bold to qualify as "good" operas, whereas it is always unmistakably— yea, infuriatingly—absent in "bad" ones, regardless of their national origin.)

Dargomyzhsky's role in this rough overview is colored, moreover, by distinctive traits of his timing, manifested in a high rate of harmonic and textural change that makes of operatic recitative—especially in *The Stone Guest*—the norm for musical unfolding, and consequently eliminates text repetition, while "numbers," organized into texturally unified melodic periods and therefore featuring a more stable orchestral accompaniment, become exceptional and, given this peculiar embedding, produce an effect of excessive length, although taken in themselves, such vestigial "numbers" are usually brief enough and entirely dispense with time-consuming vocal embellishments. The impression that such a novel sense of compressed timing was to make on Stravinsky may be inferred from the following excerpts from *The Stone Guest:* the opening scene of act 1, starting at the very beginning. I should add that the initial orchestral measures return a couple of more times during the scene, but within the recitative itself there is no repetition at all, and occasional snippets of tunes, coupled with their particular—and therefore singled-out—accompaniments, do occur, but no more than once each. You will notice that two such passages have been bracketed in example 1. The characters are Don Juan and Leporello. I sense a clear-cut connection here between the high-speed timing, the predominantly duple meter, the sporadic appearances of patterned accompaniments and throw-away tune fragments and Stravinsky's *Mavra*. That connection, it seems to me, is more explicit than any such link to Tchaikovsky or to Glinka, as suggested in the dedication of Stravinsky's little opera. Besides, Stravinksy intended *Mavra* to evoke, and point benign fun at, "provincial" Russian opera of the 1870s, as he remarked at the time *Mavra* was being recorded in Toronto. (What he could have meant by "provincial" is ambiguous: he may have

Example 1: Aleksandr Dargomyzhsky, *The Stone Guest*.

Ex. 1 (cont.)

referred to operatic practice outside Saint Petersburg and Moscow or to the more
"unurban" characteristics of Russian composers of that time, vis-à-vis their Western European counterparts.) There are other reminders here as well: the off-beat,
sforzato-secco cadence as a kind of orchestral punctuation is to imbue the Octet, for
example, and the chromatic descent of the vocal contour in the second bracketed

Example 2: Igor Stravinsky, *Oedipus Rex.* Text by J. Cocteau; translated into Latin by J. Danielou. Copyright 1927 by Edition Russe de Musique; renewed 1952. Copyright and renewal assigned to Boosey & Hawkes, Inc. Revised version copyright 1949, 1950 by Boosey & Hawkes, Inc.; renewed 1976, 1978. English translation copyright 1949, 1956, (1981), (1982) by Boosey & Hawkes, Inc.

measures may be reflected in the Shepherd's line between rehearsals 148 and 149 in *Oedipus Rex* (ex. 2). There are also inferrable derivations on a larger scale: a comparison of overtures to Dargomyzhsky's opera *Rusalka* and to *Mavra* shows similar helter-skelter parades of tunes or themes in apparent disconnection to one another, or even within themselves, so that both pieces seem to achieve a fair degree of incoherence—though in Stravinsky's case the effect was intentional and satiric. *Mavra,* in any event, was seen by Stravinsky, with special affection, as a link to his early youth. It was also the last extended Russian text that he set.

There is another curious thread running through this bit of history; in its odd and arbitrary way, it represents a resource shared by Russian composers for a specific illustrative purpose. Even Stravinsky is part of this chain, although by the time he employed this resource—uniquely, in his experience, so far as I can tell—it had lost both its novelty and its Russian contextual tag. Starting with Glinka, who used it in 1842 in *Ruslan and Lyudmila,* the whole-tone collection is explicitly stated—either linearly (most often as a bass line) or as parallel augmented triads— in association with "the bad guys" or to highlight something mysterious, or to signify terrifying emotions enacted or implied on the stage. *The Stone Guest* features it at considerable length when that petrified gentleman makes his unexpected appearance; it is used by Tchaikovsky in his last opera, *Iolanta,* to underline that young girl's fright when she first gains her eyesight (Kalmus reprint of the "Moscow" edition, pp. 317–19). Rimsky's *Golden Cockerel* abounds in it as a basis for sequences by the yard (ex. 3). Stravinsky uses it only in the Dance of the Earth at the end of part 1 of *The Rite of Spring,* where it has neither programmatic nor terrifying purposes, but serves the function of an ostinato (rehearsals 75–78).

If there is one quality that has thus far remained conspicuously undefined, but has been mentioned often enough, some effort at its elucidation is at this point due. For our general purposes, therefore, "Russian" tunes, or tunes that "sound Russian" may be defined, to an incomplete degree, at best, as sharing the following characteristics: a strongly metricized accentual structure—i.e., each beat is stressed—and predominantly coinciding meter and rhythm; frequent contour leaps of interval class 5 and frequent confinement of contour spans within that interval class; ornamentation (upper neighbors, for instance) by means of patterned rhythmic groupings, so that a tune primarily in quarters might include either groups of an eighth and two sixteenths or simply eighths; lastly, pitch repetition geared toward metric stress. I do not hereby allude to those melismatic orientalisms and manneristic exoticisms that were increasingly to permeate the nationalistic efforts of the *kuchkisti;* the tunes I am considering in terms of the stated characteristics are mainly diatonic. This attempted definition brings to mind a remark in something I wrote long ago, in which my locution "a bit of Russia in its rhythm," referring to the earliest sketch for Stravinsky's Variations, has led to a good bit of ribbing. Perhaps this is the right moment to put that description to the

Example 3: Nikolay Rimsky-
Korsakov, *The Golden
Cockerel*.

Ex. 3 (cont.)

Example 4: Igor Stravinsky, Variations, sketch. Reproduced by permission of the Paul Sacher foundation.

test (ex. 4). Certainly the opening pentad could be linked to the traits listed above, and if the succeeding heptad includes a few bold leaps, its rhythmic continuity is still not hard to associate with other "Russian" tunes we have heard—even if they were not twelve-tone tunes!

Let us now consider the missing documentation mentioned earlier. It is of two kinds: (1) work done by Stravinsky for his theory lessons, and as Rimsky's private composition student; (2) compositions and other professional work accomplished once Stravinsky had ended his studies. Among the latter, probably the single most interesting buried treasure is the work apportioned in 1912–13 by Diaghilev to Stravinsky and Ravel for the completion and restoration of Mussorgsky's *Khovanshchina*. If Stravinsky's part in this enterprise should ever come to light, it will show how much he may have striven for "authenticity" in Mussorgsky's sense. (I have recently seen a couple of pages of Ravel's score and found them lacking in any immediately inferrable connection to Mussorgsky; they looked simply like Ravel, complete with assorted *glissandi*.) What little we know to any precise degree about the work Stravinsky did with Rimsky-Korsakov we can gather only from reported autobiographical statements by Stravinsky. These mention that Rimsky gave him Beethoven piano sonatas and quartets to orchestrate, as well as Schubert marches, but the pieces assigned are nowhere identified, nor, therefore, are the constraints for these exercises (if any) specified. Only one work of Rimsky's, excerpts from which were used in this connection, is actually named: the opera *Pan Voyevoda*. Stravinsky would be given some pages of piano reduction to orchestrate, and then the results would be compared to the pertinent places in Rimsky's recently completed score. Our immediate questions—for example, as to which pages, or as to what kinds of explanation Rimsky offered to show why their respective scorings were different, or, above all, concerning the deftness or ineptitude of Stravinsky's versions—obviously have to remain unanswered, at least for the time being. One may conclude, at any rate, that these were primarily orchestration lessons; only in one place is there any reference to a composition assignment: Stravinsky's autobiography comments on Rimsky's lucidity in instructing him in the principles of sonata-allegro construction, and says that Stravinsky was enjoined to compose the first part of a sonatina under Rimsky's supervision. Such skimpy descriptions yield practically no clues as to the emulative efforts by the pupil, even if the teacher's own habits and predilections (and therefore also those of orchestration) must have played a predominant part in this pedagogic venture, so that the larger—or largest—questions are bound to concern both the extent to which Stravinsky may have seen through the gimcrack surfaces of Rimsky's music and the time at which he came to realize consciously how poor that music was.

It is easy to infer that Rimsky's role in Stravinsky's early life was more personal than directly musical, though Stravinsky probably would not have seen it in this light at the time. Rimsky's kindliness and generosity made of him a substitute father for Stravinsky, especially after his own father's death in 1902. It makes sense, then, to see Stravinsky's glowing, if also limited, accounts of his studies with Rimsky as motivated by personal affection. A cooler assessment, based on Rimsky's music, would more likely suggest a rather doctrinaire and hidebound teacher. Given a generally crude and patchy compositional usage, despite all the razzle-dazzle effects, and in view of Rimsky's narrow-minded and somewhat autocratic manner toward composers not directly within his sphere of influence, one is led to wonder what palpably beneficial consequences such a model might have produced for Stravinsky's emerging compositional practice. A gauge of the strained relation between Rimsky-Korsakov and the musical world beyond his own domain may be found in the following quotation from Rimsky's autobiography, describing his impressions of Tchaikovsky's *Iolanta*:

> I heard *Iolanta* at a rehearsal and found it one of Tchaikovsky's feeblest compositions. To my mind, everything in it is unsuccessful—beginning with impudent borrowings like Anton Rubinstein's melody [= song] "Open wide my prison" and ending with the orchestration which in this particular case Tchaikovsky had somehow written upside-down: music suitable for strings had been allotted to wind instruments, and vice versa, and hence it occasionally sounds even fantastic in the most unsuitable passages (the introduction, for instance, scored for some unknown reason for the wind instruments alone).

There is a familiar ring to criticism of this kind, but, given the ingenuity and orchestral resourcefulness amply in evidence in that score—from beginning to end—Rimsky's dismissal smacks of outright envy. Now, an examination of a few selected passages from works by Rimsky-Korsakov that are assumed to have been familiar to Stravinsky should help us gain a clearer insight about the precise ways in which his maturing compositional modus operandi may have been influenced by his teacher. The most obvious excerpt to begin with might be the middle movement of Rimsky's Sinfonietta on Russian Themes, inasmuch as its primary material is the same tune on which Stravinsky wrote the *Khorovod* in *The Firebird*. However, there is no connection between any aspects of either composer's treatment of that tune. Rimsky's movement is endlessly repetitious, episodic (as if he were writing variations which, it then turns out, he is not), and the tune's harmonization is itself astonishingly flat (ex. 5). The whole piece appears, moreover, to suffer from acute motivitis, which is to say that the persistent use of a few motivically derived offshoots of the tune is sufficiently lacking in ingenuity so as to guarantee monotony. Stravinsky's *Khorovod,* shown here in its arrangement for the 1919 Suite, on the other hand, reveals several procedural characteristics that seem a fair distance beyond the reaches of Rimsky-Korsakov's imagination (ex. 6). For one thing, the tune is shaped to avoid bland repetitiveness after the third measure, by transposing its opening ascent down a minor third, thereby facilitating the descent to an F♯, now harmonized on the dominant. The continuation, spinning out registrally diverse derivatives of the tune, lands on a harmony from which a simple bass motion to F♯ could have led to a repetition of the tune. Instead, Stravinsky's choice is to turn the top line's G♯ horn doubling into a similar G♯ in the violins, and to embark on a section of the piece whose newness is made manifest simultaneously by orchestral, articulative, and thematic changes, with a corresponding shift of tempo. We need go no further than to notice that G♯ pitch-link to recognize an instance of a bridging device that was to be used throughout Stravinsky's career. But I do not mean to suggest that pitch-links of this kind are necessarily to be derived from Rimsky models, or from any of his teaching; in fact, I doubt that this device came from any one exclusive source, or that Stravinsky's falling back upon its habitual employment could be attributed to any one composer's example or influence.

Among surface traits passed along—at least temporarily—from Rimsky's practice to Stravinsky's, there is a species of harmonic trick whose effect is to propel successions along symmetrical paths—i.e., by common interval or intervallic patterning—and to provide thereby an illusion of harmonic remoteness, while often actually remaining within easy distance from wherever the mechanism started. You may recall that example 3—the measures from *The Golden Cockerel*—goes through just such a cycle: the whole-tone bass descent supports an arpeggiating tune that proceeds by two-measure units successively transposed a major third down, until

Example 5: Nikolay Rimsky-Korsakov, Sinfonietta (rehearsal *A*).

Claudio Spies

Example 6: Igor Stravinsky, *Khorovod.*

the circular motion is completed. Notice that all elements in this patterning are in absolute and unvarying concordance with the metrical setup—an annoyingly pervasive trait, as we shall soon see. Another instance of a particular sequential trick—of whose general abundance in the music of Rimsky-Korsakov, the less remembered, the better—may be seen in the opening measures of the opera *Christmas Eve* (ex. 7): here root-position triads move so that while the bass descends by alternating major and minor thirds, the simultaneities are registered so that the top line describes an ascent by alternating intervals 2 and 3. Rimsky stops just short of getting back to E in the bass, possibly because he realized in the nick of time that he would have been in trouble if he had allowed the cycle to continue *beyond* that E, or because he knew he could invoke a different harmonic trick to get back to a tonic triad, even if it were to have no E in the bass. So, as you may observe, he moves his bass to F, prolongs an unconvincingly resolved unresolved harmony on that F for nine long measures and, just before the page turn, resolves it—or at least resolves the bass by moving it to E. Could anyone not guess the further pursuit of this mechanical enterprise? Suffice it to say that it takes another fourteen measures of such silliness before that predictable low B is reached. But I suspect I may have made my point.

Example 7: Nikolay Rimsky-Korsakov, *Christmas Eve.*

Ex. 7 (cont.)

Let us now see how Stravinsky makes such a cyclic trick turn to his advantage in *The Firebird* (ex. 8). The tremolando strings leading into the ballet's second scene—in the Suites this music connects the Lullaby to the Final Hymn, and therefore has a different bass line, as well as doubled note values in the upper parts, until the last five measures—exhibit a chromatic descent including all pitch classes in the uppermost violins, while a compound bass line rises in staggered patternings of alternating intervals 2 and 3. The resulting dyadic simultaneities of that bass line consequently alternate between intervals 4 and 3, and cumulatively the two octotonic collections based on F♯ are thereby articulated. The inner parts, however, obliterate any merely mechanical notion in our perception of the passage, since they are devised to collaborate in not producing stacks either of triads in any exclusive position, or any other particular vertical configuration with any discernible regularity. What Stravinsky's procedure shows, then, is that the employment of this kind of harmonic trick-mechanism may nevertheless be cleverly disguised to veil predictable successions, and may furthermore end in an unforeseen arrival. What it also specifically implies is an early context for what Stravinsky would often call "composing with intervals."

If the notion that Rimsky-Korsakov and Stravinsky also shared compositional procedures or techniques in the large sense strikes us perforce as essentially suspect, we are obliged nonetheless to recognize the peculiar local significance of Rimsky's predilection for the tritone and for putting this obsessive infatuation—as

Example 8: Igor Stravinsky, *The Firebird.*

well as for its harmonic compounding at t³ or its complement—constantly to the proof. One blatant instance, from the opera *The Legend of the Invisible City of Kityezh,* should suffice without need for further comment (ex. 9). As for the effect of this predilection on Stravinsky's music, we need think only of the opening measure of the *Firebird* Suite of 1919, and its manifold extensions on the first page of the score to infer that the tritone has been granted "most favored interval" status throughout the ballet.

Obvious though it be, by now, that isolated surface features of Rimsky's compositional practice found their way—in their own way—into the roster of Stravinsky's resources at the time of *The Firebird* and other youthful works, mention should nevertheless be made of a few additional characteristics of this sort. One of them involves the frequent restatement of a given melodic idea within a short time-span, sometimes with harmonic changes for achieving alternation or balance among units and their multiples, and sometimes without even such simple harmonic change. It occurs so often in Rimsky's larger works that it would be

Claudio Spies

pointless to pick out one particular instance. Its direct effect on Stravinsky's music may be gauged in *The Firebird*'s Final Hymn, whose eleven complete statements of a tune (with additional segments thereof interspersed) maintain that tune's unmistakable identity despite rerhythmicization, change of tempo, and momentary transposition. Another place in the same Suite where this procedure may be seen operating in somewhat crasser terms is between numbers 15 and 21 of the Infernal

Example 9: Nikolay Rimsky-Korsakov, *The Invisible City of Kityezh.*

Ex. 9 (cont.)

Dance: here persistent two-measure units, coupled with all the internal repetition, become tiresome, although the effect desired is to lead into the next section.

It would be difficult to imagine Stravinsky's rhythmic and metric techniques as being in any way influenced by his teacher's practices in that domain. In fact, it is easier to understand Stravinsky's usage as an effort to do the very opposite of Rimsky-Korsakov, and for the best of reasons, to boot. So, when we come across time-signature changes by the measure, in *The Invisible City of Kityezh* (ex. 10), we observe soon enough that they are merely measures of equal length whose internal organization is alternately three half notes and two dotted halves, with every means of stressing every beat in evidence, so as to drive the point home. Likewise, in the same opera, the passage in which 9/8 is arranged in groups of measures whose internal eighth-note makeup is, successively, 3+3+3 (four measures); 2+3+2+2 (two measures); 2+2+2+3 (six measures)—and, a few measures later, with the same successive subdivisions, allotted to the same measure groups (ex. 11)—involves no more than rigorously repetitive patterns whose slight internal changes are neither counterbalanced nor metrically counterpointed. The source for such shifting metric subdivisions must lie in Russian folktunes or in poetry—or in both—and inasmuch as these sources produced such vastly different results in Stravinsky's music, no more need for now be said.

Example 10: Nikolay Rimsky-Korsakov, *The Invisible City of Kityezh.*

Example 11: *The Invisible City of Kityezh.*

94

Ex. II (cont.)

(continued)

Claudio Spies

Ex. II (cont.)

Example 12: Igor Stravinsky,
Final Hymn, *The Firebird*.

Ex. 12 (cont.)

There is a simple, rather hackneyed means for smoothing over surface continuity between contiguous phrases. It is in itself unremarkable, but its echo-aping is used in the above-named opera with such oppressive frequency that it could be perceived as a trap into which Stravinsky fell unwittingly at the beginning of the Final Hymn (ex. 12), although the echo may here be taken to open the upper register for the tune. In *Kityezh*, such echoing patterns are set up at the very outset (ex. 13), continuing well beyond what is shown here, and return dutifully—even in the same oboe—with the recurrence of this music.

One last surface device consists either of filling in chromatically by means of parallel harmonic slithers, or half-tone transpositions effecting local harmonic switches or emphases. Three places in *Kityezh* exemplify Rimsky's procedure: the first (ex. 14) moves by half-tone both in parallel and contrary motion; the next two (exx. 15a and 15b) feature chromatic parallel slithers, prolonging one harmony, or moving over pedals.

97

Claudio Spies

Example 13: Nikolay Rimsky-
Korsakov, *The Invisible City of
Kityezh*.

98

Example 14: Nikolay Rimsky-
Korsakov, *The Invisible City of
Kityezh.*

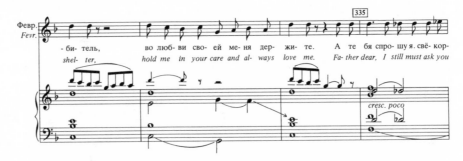

Claudio Spies

Example 15a: *The Invisible City of Kityezh.*

Example 15b: *The Invisible City of Kityezh.*

IOO

Example 16: Igor Stravinsky, *Perséphone*. Text by André Gide. Copyright 1934 by Edition Russe de Musique; renewed 1961. Revised version copyright 1950 by Boosey & Hawkes, Inc. Renewed 1978 by Boosey & Hawkes, Inc.

You will probably agree with me at this point that it might have been preferable for Rimsky to have composed an opera on "The Inaudible City of Kityezh"!

Both of these procedures are combined within a few measures in act 1 of Stravinsky's *Nightingale* (pp. 23–25, one before rehearsal 21).

By some strange quirk, the chromatic slithering device finds its way into later works as well: in *Perséphone,* for instance, (ex. 16) the phrase ending before 20 combines a three-part chromatic slither in the female voices with a contravening upward motion in the clarinets within the same register, while a little later (ex. 17) the same slither takes on a more distinctly cadential aspect; and in *Orpheus,* between 72 and 74 (ex. 18) slithering occurs in registral, rhythmic, and instrumental independence, giving rise to a discontinuous pitch line between both participating strands, and the "cadential" impression is conveyed chiefly by the bass line.

Example 17: Igor Stravinsky, *Perséphone*. Text by André Gide. Copyright 1934 by Edition Russe de Musique; renewed 1961. Revised version copyright 1950 by Boosey & Hawkes, Inc. Renewed 1978 by Boosey & Hawkes, Inc.

Ex. 17 (cont.)

A connecting, or perhaps "liquidating," function is assigned to the trumpets' slither just before the return in the Tango (p. 14, before rehearsal 6), but here the slither is also motivically derived, and comes as less of a surprise.

The one composition written after 1910 in which Stravinsky appears to absorb Rimsky's influence in more than isolated spots, and in which he ventures into very hazardous territory without appearing to be concerned for compositional coherence or for continuity generated by musical rather than poetic materials, is the cantata *Zvezdoliki*. Harmonic curiosities, actually made up of pretty straightforward motions, but heavily loaded with "extra" pitches of an ornamental nature, lead to a degree of density comparable, perhaps, only to the twelve-part string episodes in the late Variations. These oddities appear to be used for their local effect

Example 18: Igor Stravinsky, *Orpheus.* Copyright 1947, 1948 by Boosey & Hawkes, Inc. Renewed 1974, 1975.

only, and to contribute little to an understanding of the piece's overall unity. One place, however, features an intervallic chain over a deftly asymmetrical bass whose result is that remarkable succession of wind simultaneities (rehearsals 8 and 9) that make one think—for not quite the right reasons—of the ending of the Symphony in C. A schematized representation of top and bottom lines will highlight the intervallic links and overlaps, and also indicate the asymmetrical biases (ex. 19).

In assessing its overall effect on Stravinsky, Rimsky-Korsakov's music may be more accurately judged a deterrent, rather than an encouragement, to emulative efforts. We have seen that a number of surface details support this view. At the same time, however, one is led to wonder whether Stravinsky, in his determination to avoid the larger-scale episodic and sequence-laden constructions of his teacher,

Example 19: Igor Stravinsky, *Zvezdoliki*. Copyright 1971 renewed by Rob. Forberg–P. Jurgenson. Reprinted by permission of C. F. Peters Corporation, sole selling agents for Rob. Forberg.

might not have hit upon simply another way of dealing with episodic construction, and might not similarly have substituted dependence on ostinati for his teacher's incurable infatuation with literally repetitive designs, sequential or not. Furthermore, the "patchwork" processes in composing that our very limited glances at some pages of Stravinsky's sketch materials have so far allowed us to confirm, in addition to his documented difficulty in achieving proper timing and balance in the proportions of certain last movements—the Sonata for Two Pianos and the "Basler" Concerto for Strings come to mind—could be conjectured to arise from an effort to "translate" Rimsky's harmonic mechanisms and their predictable piecemeal exhaustion (by saturation and surfeit) into terms of a particular kind of continuity, with all its attendant considerations regarding contrast, alternation, use of refrains, strophic construction, etc.—an effort whose origin would then easily have justified the surprising degree of skittishness shown by Stravinsky in handling larger sections of thematic elaboration or development. (I am referring here to the first movements of the Sonata for Two Pianos and the Symphony in C—two unique instances, respectively, of half and full-fledged "development sections" among Stravinsky's mature works.) It is tempting, therefore, to think of Stravinsky as working out his own manner in defiance, as it were, of Rimsky's, and, for the period up to the end of World War I, at least, this interpretation may well apply with some accuracy to Stravinsky's predominantly Russian works. Still, to construe the large-scale composing-out of tritone relations, for instance, in a later work as any sort of offshoot of Rimsky-Korsakov would be ludicrous; the Concerto for Two Pianos shares nothing with that source.

One name has up to now somewhat conspicuously been left unmentioned. That omission may be defended by the circumstance that Scriabin's influence on Stravinsky's music is limited quite specifically to the Four Piano Etudes of 1908. The later, more mystical—or, if you prefer, steamier—Scriabin exercised no attraction for Stravinsky's ear—in fact, he detested him and his music in equal measure. Even if the harmonic vocabulary of *The Firebird* could be perceived as reminiscent of Scriabin's, its orchestral garb is more patterned to textural sectioning—it is, after all, dance music—and less inclined to revel in surface glitter for its own sake. Besides, Stravinsky could rely on his teacher for cues in extracting and employing the octotonic collection, without needing to invoke anyone else's tritonal monomania.

An early inkling as to a more pervasive influence on Stravinsky's music is offered in the opening measures (ex. 20) of *Faun and Shepherdess,* composed while he was still studying with Rimsky. Were it not for the fifth measure—inserted, I suspect, as an afterthought—there would be nothing likely to challenge an hypothetical attribution of this music to Tchaikovsky. From the rhythmically patterned, sequential rise in the accompaniment to the contrabass's change to *arco,* just before the cadence, or from the delayed entrance of wind doublings for highlighting the new dynamic to the overlap between violins and the voice in reaching for the higher F, this passage reveals how professionally familiar Stravinsky was with Tchaikovsky's ways of handling local continuity and registral progression, as well as with his characteristic refinements of orchestral writing and the placement of a vocal line in an instrumental ambience. An even more solid clue is suggested by the absence of any discernible Rimskyan traits in this piece, a circumstance likely to have caused some discomfiture. Moreover, given the particular, strongly derived flavor of several such passages in *Faun and Shepherdess,* it is rather tempting to speculate about the relative disappearance of Tchaikovsky's influence in most of the music Stravinsky composed between, roughly, 1908 and 1918.

A surer perspective on specific ways to perceive Tchaikovsky's influence may be gained by our adopting the expedient of a few categories into which aspects of a compositional surface, or technical details establishing the context for a surface, can be subsumed. One such category could comprise component elements, taken in themselves—or lifted out of their immediate contexts—as a criterion for comparisons. Take, for example, the passage from Stravinsky's Violin Concerto in example 21 and compare its alternating groups of two thirty-seconds to the similar accompanying sixteenths in a passage from the opera *Iolanta* (ex. 22). In itself, such an accompaniment is perhaps not startling, yet is is not so commonplace as to elude notice, and while Stravinsky's viola line acts as a sustaining counterbalance to the solo violin's recitation, Tchaikovsky brings in brass instruments to support a change in dynamics only after this texture has been set up to accompany the vocal bass.

In the case of Anne's B-minor aria, from act 1, scene 3 in *The Rake's Progress* (ex.

Example 20: Igor Stravinsky,
Faun and Shepherdess.
Copyright 1964 by M. P.
Belaieff. Used by permission
of C. F. Peters Corporation.

Claudio Spies

Example 21: Igor Stravinsky, Concerto for Violin. Copyright B. Schott's Soehne, Mainz 1931. Copyright renewed 1959. All rights reserved. Used by permission of European American Music Distributors Corporation, sole U.S. agent for B. Schott's Soehne.

Ex. 21 (cont.)

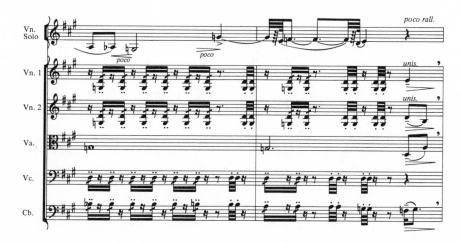

23), two accompanimental components are strongly reminiscent of Tchaikovsky's operas: the elegantly layered, varyingly registered string texture, and the bassoon's line, woven around, and in terms of, the soprano line. (There are several instances of both features in *Eugene Onegin;* one need only recall Lensky's aria in act 3, or various places in Tatiana's Letter Scene.) Sometimes a singly reiterated textural component may serve the purpose of accompanying, especially in contexts where ostinato elements are necessarily scarce, and brings about a recollection of Tchaikovskyan models; in the female dancer's brief variation, during the Pas-de-Deux from *Agon* (ex. 24), the patterned rhythmicization of the unchanging string

Example 22: Pyotr Ilyich Tchaikovsky, *Iolanta.*

Claudio Spies

Ex. 22 (cont.)

Example 23: Igor Stravinsky, *The Rake's Progress*. Libretto by W. H. Auden and Chester Kallman. Copyright 1949, 1950, 1951 by Boosey & Hawkes, Inc.; renewed 1976, 1977, 1979. Reprinted by permission.

Ex. 23 (cont.)

ca- ress, And may thou qui——et find his heart,—— al- though

Example 24: Igor Stravinsky, *Agon*. Copyright 1957 by Boosey & Hawkes, Inc. Renewed 1985. Reprinted by permission of Boosey & Hawkes, Inc.

Ex. 24 (cont.)

simultaneities simply spells "ballet accompaniment" while acting as a backdrop for a set-unfolding in the flutes. In a related manner, passages whose rhythms and contours might justify an assumption that Stravinsky was winking at later or earlier eighteenth-century models, nevertheless reveal some recognizably Tchai-kovskyan component. In *Orpheus,* for instance, the F-minor Air de Danse (ex. 25) has a layer of oboes over the harp's "oompah" accompaniment. The effect is a trifle bizarre—as if Bach were being heard through Tchaikovsky's ear! Even *Pulcinella,*

Example 25: Igor Stravinsky, *Orpheus*. Copyright 1947, 1948 by Boosey & Hawkes, Inc. Renewed 1974, 1975.

using assorted tidbits by Pergolesi—or whoever—incorporates reminders of Tchaikovsky: a bassoon solo interspersed with pizzicato strings is like something embedded from another piece—a musical meteorite (ex. 26a)—and the beginning of "Se tu m'ami" sounds like the Italian opera Tchaikovsky neglected to write (ex. 26b).

Another category involves apparent, momentary "quotes" from Tchaikovsky's music. These act in a startling, somewhat disturbing fashion, temporarily

disrupting one's perception of continuity. The effect is, approximately, to make one ask oneself, "Where have I heard this before?" or, if there should be no need, to induce an "Aha!" of recognition. One such place, for my ear, has always been the seeming cadence in the Dirge-Canons of *In memoriam Dylan Thomas* (exx. 27a and 27b). Notice that the second occurrence, in the string quartet, is at t^{10}. In *Romeo and Juliet,* the two occurrences of a similar cadential device are related by t^{11} (exx. 28a and 28b). Now notice that the transposition level of Tchaikovsky's *first* such cadence coincides with Stravinsky's *second,* and that the registral distributions match, at least half-way.

A more obvious instance is found at the opening of Stravinsky's Ode, whose brass simultaneities, in their long-short-long rhythmic apportionment, are very similar to the brass at the beginning of *Francesca da Rimini* (ex. 29), yet even more so at m. 60, inasmuch as the interval of the top trumpet's neighboring motion is now a half-step. (This particular resemblance may invoke offshoots, since that neighboring motif is common to a good many of Stravinsky's compositions. It is more appropriate, however, for present purposes, to avoid any such easy generalization.)

Before going on to the category dealing with Stravinsky's actual use of Tchaikovsky's materials, and therefore also Tchaikovsky's techniques, there should be one brief historical interpolation—an aside, as it were—to point out that from 1919 on, all the ballets Stravinsky was to compose during the rest of his life were written in adherence to certain Tchaikovskyan notions. It is incorrect to assume

Example 26b: Igor
Stravinsky, *Pulcinella* (after
Giambattista Pergolesi).
Copyright 1924 by Edition
Russe de Musique; renewed
1952. Revised version
copyright 1949 by Boosey &
Hawkes, Inc.; renewed 1976.

that Tchaikovsky's influence made itself felt only after Stravinsky had orchestrated two numbers from *The Sleeping Beauty* (that had for some reason been omitted from earlier productions), commissioned for Diaghilev's London revival of 1921. *Pulcinella* preceded that piece of work, and, as we have seen, exhibits some unmistakable Tchaikovskyisms. In view of Stravinsky's unshaken subsequent fidelity to "number" ballets—no matter whether also provided with a plot, or merely a succession of dances—and to episodic construction by means of textures elaborating the most elegant and varied accompaniments, it is surprising that the ballets *prior* to *Pulcinella* seem to disregard, or disavow, such Tchaikovskyan precedents.

Claudio Spies

Example 27a: Igor
Stravinsky, *In memoriam
Dylan Thomas* (song "Do Not
Go Gentle": poem by Dylan
Thomas). Copyright 1954 by
Boosey & Hawkes, Inc.; re-
newed 1982. Reprinted by
permission. From *Collected
Poems of Dylan Thomas;* by
permission of J. M. Dent and
Sons.

116

Example 27b: Igor
Stravinsky, *In memoriam
Dylan Thomas* (song "Do Not
Go Gentle": poem by Dylan
Thomas). Copyright 1954 by
Boosey & Hawkes, Inc.; re-
newed 1982. Reprinted by
permission. From *Collected
Poems of Dylan Thomas;* by
permission of J. M. Dent and
Sons.

Claudio Spies

Example 28a: Pyotr Ilyich Tchaikovsky, *Romeo and Juliet*.

Example 28b: Pyotr Ilyich Tchaikovsky, *Romeo and Juliet*.

118

Ex. 28b (cont.)

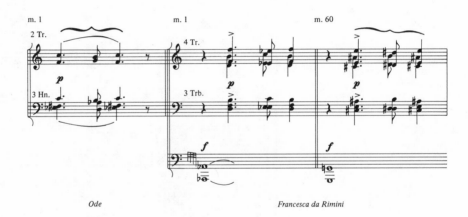

Ode   Francesca da Rimini

Those ballets belong to the decade between 1908 and 1918 mentioned earlier; we shall have one further occasion to allude to that period.

There can be little question as to the powerful stimulus, nevertheless, provided by the labor of orchestrating those two numbers from *The Sleeping Beauty*. It was evidently the impetus leading to *Le baiser de la fée* and *Apollo*, even if seven years were to elapse before Stravinsky was to undertake these works. Of all the wonders wrought by that odd symbiosis whereby *Le baiser de la fée* was made to contain some of the best music Tchaikovsky never composed, it will be enough for us now to glance at one tiny but telling detail in scene 3. The music on which the *Doppio movimento* episode at 143 (ex. 30a) is based is the Album Leaf, op. 19, no. 3 (ex. 30b). For four measures, Stravinsky limits himself to scoring for a wind sextet, albeit with several notes abbreviated, so as to ensure clear articulation and separation. From m. 5 on, however, he adds a counterpoint by way of a scalar rise in the violins that soon becomes the highest instrumental voice. Now, when the syncopating sequences begin in m. 8, Stravinsky retains his new upper line, articulated in homophony with the syncopation, but whereas Tchaikovsky's lowest voice moves downward on each accented eighth in the dyadic groups, Stravinsky breaks that pattern in the second bassoon's iterated G and the dyadic *descent* to F♯ (rather than moving from E to F♯). The reason for this change may well reside in the A–A♯ motion—allowing for half-step contrary motion between outer parts—but also in the consistently deployed half-step motion within each dyad for the lower bassoon. It is a matter of the differentiable timbre in that bassoon's line that induced Stravinsky to opt for intervallic consistency here; in the piano piece, however, the

Example 30a: Igor Stravinsky, *Le baiser de la fée*. Copyright 1952, 1954 by Boosey & Hawkes, Inc. Renewed 1980, 1982. Reprinted by permission.

Ex. 30a (cont.)

(continued)

Ex. 30a (cont.)

G–F♯ would have been quite inconsistent. Furthermore, Stravinsky gradually fills in registral space for the strings, by first doubling at the lower octave and then tripling at one more octave's remove—thereby gaining a typically Tchaikovskyan string sound—while his top line reaches its highest point: the appositeness of this counterpoint is a gauge of Stravinsky's extraordinarily skillful adoption of his partner's personal technique.

The opening measures of *Le baiser de la fée* (ex. 31) bring up a more peculiar and, at first, less apparently explicit connection. Tchaikovsky's opera *The Little Slippers,* a work based on the same story by Gogol that Rimsky was later to have the temerity to treat in his *Christmas Eve* (of unhappy memory), begins as in example 32a. Not only is there a shared design of alternating woodwinds—notably flutes doubled at one or two octaves—and strings, but a certain seepage of Tchaikovsky's exclusive tetrachordal concerns may also be observed. A schematic representation (exx. 32a, 32b, 32c, and ex. 33) of three main tunes from Tchaikovsky's overture to this opera shows successive or interlocking *2,3,2* tetrachords, leading to an eventual

Example 30b: Pyotr Ilyich
Tchaikovsky, Album Leaf, op.
19, no. 3.

inclusion of, or transformation into, *3,2,3* tetrachords. At rehearsal 1 in *Le baiser de la fée,* you will likewise see an embedded *2,3,2* tetrachord. In itself, such evidence of connectedness may seem flimsy or even capricious, but I should suggest that there is much more here than coincidence. Stravinsky knew this opera—he must have loved it—and he is very likely to have retained a lasting impression of its beginning, in view of its exclusive intervallic usage; a property of that kind, moreover, is apt to have left its mark—consciously or not, identifiably or merely "stored"—on his perceptions, no matter when that impression may have been gained. If a tag should be required for this category of linkage, the term "subliminal" may be fitting. At any rate, in going through *Le baiser de la fée,* one suspects increasingly that there might be many more connections of this sort, and that Tchaikovsky's presence may therefore be in evidence even in those tunes and passages Stravinsky attributes to himself.

A more overt transfer of registral, textural, and orchestral, as well as tempo-related traits occurs between Tchaikovsky's First Symphony and the Symphony in C: compare only the first page (ex. 34a) of Tchaikovsky's score to the first movement of Stravinsky's symphony, between rehearsal numbers 5 and 7 (ex. 34b) and you will notice that the metronomic is common to both, even if the time signature is not, and that Stravinsky's three-note motif is not only the head of Tchaikovsky's tune in retrograde, but likewise fills in the fourth G–C with stepwise downward motion, albeit in major. Then observe the similar slow-fast tempo succession at the beginning of either symphony's fourth movement, along with respectively shared motivic and melodic material, the predominant placement of such material in a

Ex. 31 (1 of 2)

Example 31: Igor Stravinsky, *Le baiser de la fée.* Copyright 1952, 1954 by Boosey & Hawkes, Inc. Renewed 1980, 1982. Reprinted by permission.

Ex. 31 (cont.)

lower register, and—most tellingly—the reappearance of the slower, introductory music in mid-movement. For your relief, however, I make no claim for any kinship between these symphonies' endings!

Example 32a: Pyotr Ilyich Tchaikovsky, *The Little Slippers*.

(continued)

Ex. 32a (cont.)

Example 32b: *The Little Slippers.*

Example 32c: *The Little Slippers.*

Example 33: *The Little Slippers.*

Example 34a: Pyotr Ilyich Tchaikovsky, Symphony no. 1.

Ex. 34a (cont.)

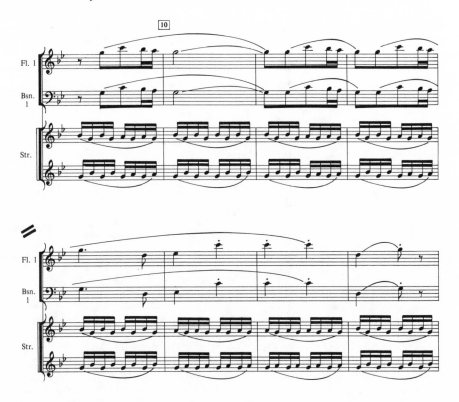

Example 34b: Igor Stravinsky, Symphony in C. Copyright Schott & Co., Ltd., London, 1948. Copyright renewed 1976. All rights reserved. Used by permission of European American Music Distributors Corporation, sole U.S. agent for Schott & Co., Ltd.

(continued)

Ex. 34b (cont.)

In order to take stock of some contour characteristics, consider the tune beginning at the fourth measure of rehearsal 6 (*Moderato con moto*) in Tchaikovsky's *Hamlet*. Its schematization in example 35 will highlight both rhythmic and intervallic consistencies, as well as stepwise ascents and descents. The upper layer is conjoined with the lower, and only the octave-transferred G♯ in the second last measure prevents the final C♯ from being articulated in yet a third registral position. As it is, the half-note rhythmic break in the sixth measure appears redundant, and the two subsequent measures are too alike for comfort. But perhaps the besetting fault is in the parallel scale descents in both tune and bass line. Be that as it may, aspects of the rhythmic structure and contour design in this melody are keenly reminiscent of Stravinsky, as two relatives among his tunes may prove. First, the fugue subject in the Ode (beginning at rehearsal 2)—presented and accompanied in such a way as to suggest anything but the onset of a fugal segment—and its schematized form (ex. 36) again reveal a symmetrical layout, sequentially designed to convey two registral strands, and ending on the same pitch on which it began— although that final C is briefly given a different harmonic function. It is interesting to note that this tune is altered (mainly in its rhythmic-metric continuity) in each of its eight subsequent appearances, probably in an effort to contravene its symmetry. Secondly, a section from the Pas-de-Deux in *Danses concertantes* contains a melody

Example 35: Pyotr Ilyich
Tchaikovsky, *Hamlet.*

Example 36: Igor Stravinsky,
Ode. Copyright Schott &
Co., Ltd., London, 1947.
Copyright assigned to Associated Music Publishers Inc.,
New York. Copyright as-
signed to B. Schott's
Soehne, Mainz, 1968. All
rights reserved. Used by permission of European American Music Distributors
Corporation, sole U.S. agent
for B. Schott's Soehne.

whose built-in repetitions and motivic redundancies are enough in evidence to require no additional depiction. (Cf. rehearsal 153 to the fourth measure of rehearsal 158; note that the first seventeen measures of this music are repeated.) One notices that the chromatically rising motif is transferrable between octave locations, and the trumpet's takeover at one measure after 155 produces a temporizing segment that is particularly akin to the reiterative "noodling" in the *Hamlet* tune, after the sixth measure.

Lest it be inferred from all these demonstrable links that Stravinsky's admiration for Tchaikovsky was unreserved, I shall need to take recourse, exceptionally, to an anecdote. Sometime in the latter 1950s, Stravinsky conducted the C-Major Serenade for String Orchestra in New York, from where, a few days later, he would leave for Europe. I was among the friends who saw him off at the then Idlewild Airport, and I took that opportunity to ask him about certain off-beat accents I had noticed in his performance, which I could not find in my score. (I innocently thought Stravinsky might have known of certain dynamic details that may have been "authentic" enough, but that had been left out of the various editions of this work.) I remember that he answered with a big grin, saying (in French) that although he *adored* the piece, he felt compelled to do something about its characteristically predictable phrase structure. "You know: $1 + 1 = 2$; $2 + 2 = 4$; $4 + 4 = 8$; $8 + 8 = 16$ . . . and so on, and so on. One *has* to do something to make it more interesting!"

He very much enjoyed conducting the *Little Russian* Symphony too, but I regret never having had a chance to hear his performance of the *Pathétique*. A few of us, in fact, are apt to remember the Columbia Records project that would have had Stravinsky conduct all six symphonies; unfortunately it never saw fruition.

A few instances of Tchaikovskyisms that are so recognizable as to need no detailed description or reference to any single source will comprise the second last of our categories. For reasons made obvious at the beginning of this paper, these occurrences will be taken from two of Stravinsky's operas: *The Rake's Progress* and *Oedipus Rex.* Although it has often enough been said of the former that it was largely inspired by *Così fan tutte,* and although the specifiable references to that work are both numerous and very easy to place, it was actually a performance of *Idomeneo* in Boston, in 1947, that planted the seed for this allegedly Mozartean enterprise. What has remained shrouded in the strangest silence, however, is the plentiful evidence of Stravinsky's intimate knowledge of Tchaikovsky's operas, which comes through with impeccable precision in such places as act 2, scene 1, between rehearsals 12 and 19, where the recitative includes an independently con-trived horn line continuity, providing the main melodic matter, and where the sudden harmonic shift coinciding with the trumpet's entrance at 15 is as breath-stopping as it is Tchaikovskyan. (When he came east sometime in 1949 or '50, Stravinsky played and sang these passages for me, amid grunts and imprecations, on a piano muted almost beyond audibility, and without pronouncing a single word of the copious text. He was especially proud of the passage, and later, during rehearsals for the first production, always showed his fondness for it.) In the opening scene, the brief orchestral interlude—somewhat like a pantomime—be-tween rehearsal numbers 95 and 98 is self-explanatory and no less striking. The Trio in act 2, scene 2 (from rehearsal 131 on)—really a duet with an interrupting third voice—may speak for itself about its origin.

In *Oedipus Rex,* the rhythmic-metric balance and the restrained orchestral variety in accompanying make up the clearest references at the beginning of Oedipus' E♭ aria (at rehearsal 45) and again toward its close (at rehearsal 56). In his subsequent aria (beginning at rehearsal 83), it is the ending that most obviously evokes Tchaikovsky (from rehearsal 89 on) through the flute's and solo violin's chromatic ascent, and the deft neighboring among and between the imitative oboe and tenor—though I know of no ending by Tchaikovsky that evaporates in quite this way. Chromatic motion in outer parts is, again, the reason for selecting two more climactic moments: between rehearsals 189 and 190, and the fourth of the Messenger's cries, at 196.

Continued allusions to these two operas now brings me to a much broader conjecture concerning Stravinsky's "neoclassicism." Let us for a moment disconnect this term from all its silly pseudo-aesthetics and its prevalent journalistic inaccuracy; let us, in fact, consider the tag as no more than a pentad of nonsense syllables. We may then be in a better position to evaluate a very probable source for what the term *should* describe in Tchaikovsky's practice, for surely his Suite no. 4, also called *Mozartiana,* consisting of his expert orchestral arrangements of three piano pieces by Mozart, and of Liszt's piano transcription of the *Ave Verum*—additional angelic cascades notwithstanding—is as much an instance of this phenomenon in Tchaikovsky's terms as *Pulcinella* is in Stravinsky's. Moreover, Tchaikovsky's inclusion of unmistakable references to eighteenth-century music in two of his operas, and a Sarabande in one of his ballets, indicates a more than fleeting interest in techniques and practices of that bygone era. In act 2 of *Eugene Onegin,* the Frenchman Triquet sings congratulatory couplets to Tatiana; though the music is not acknowledged to be a quotation from any known eighteenth-century source, it may as well be thought of as such, and it must certainly have been intended to have that effect. By the same token, the Intermezzo in act 2 of *The Queen of Spades,* provided as an entertainment for guests at a ball, features a succession of choruses, dances, and duets—including a Sarabande and Tempo di Minuetto—entirely evocative of eighteenth-century models, and uninterrupted, furthermore, by any dramatic action or singing on the spectators' part. Later in the same act, the old Countess sings an air from Grétry's *Richard Coeur de Lion* to herself—all two stanzas of it—embedded within a very different musical context. In Stravinsky's music, such embeddings and contiguities could be exemplified in the "neoclassic" second movement of the Symphony in Three Movements, contained between distinctly "non-neoclassic" outer movements—for whatever the negative form of the tag might be worth.

We will indeed have come full circle in taking up our last category which comprises a few instances of Tchaikovsky's orchestration being reminiscent of Stravinsky. In the *Pas berrichon* from act 3 of *The Sleeping Beauty* (ex. 37) registral changes are enhanced by shifting the participants in each of the articulated octave sounds, although once set up, the pattern of those instrumental shifts remains constant, even after the octaves are relegated to a subsidiary role by the appearance of quite another tune in m. 11. Tchaikovsky's choices in the instrumental makeup of mm. 3–7 seem to produce greater registral disjunction than these octave sounds would themselves achieve, were they projected through greater timbral continuity. The effect is remarkably "Stravinskyan."

Again, the last dance in a brief ballet-divertimento near the beginning of act 2 in *The Maid of Orleans* (ex. 38) contains several orchestral details not ordinarily associated with Tchaikovsky's practice, but usually with Stravinsky's: the upward-moving sixteenths, beginning at m. 12, show a continuous grouping by sevens in the clarinets, and later also in the flutes, while at the same time the oboes play unison doubling groups of three; the scoring of brass instruments from m. 16 on, especially the third trombone's well-registered counterpoint to the strings' rhythm, suggests a number of better-known passages; and the very rapid alternation of groups of two sixteenths, articulated in mm. 29ff. between woodwinds, horns, and strings, might well be deemed risky in its nineteenth-century context, particularly in view of the strongly accented attacks and the lack of doubling for horns and strings.

Finally (ex. 39), at the end of the second movement of the *Little Russian* Symphony, thematic material is dissolved over the continuous march rhythm in solo timpani, with attacks in woodwinds avoiding any downbeat after m. 172, and sustaining first an off-beat attack and then, twice, on off-eighths. The last two measures wrap it up very much *alla* Stravinsky. No wonder the old gentleman loved to conduct this piece!

In summing up, then, we may construe the enduring and pervasive influence of Tchaikovsky's music on Stravinsky's works following the end of World War I as coinciding with a reevaluation in Stravinsky's mind of the meaning of Russian music for him and for his activity from that time on. Once settled in France, he soon saw the futility and impracticality of continuing to produce compositions based on Russian texts or stories or folktunes, since these would have been bound to bear the stamp of mere exotic regionalism or quaint nationalism in a cultural milieu whose notion of *chic* had by then largely bypassed that trend. If once, in the pre–World

Example 37: Pyotr Ilyich
Tchaikovsky, *Sleeping Beauty.*

(continued)

Ex. 37 (cont.)

Example 38: Pyotr Ilyich Tchaikovsky, *The Maid of Orleans*.

(continued)

Ex. 38 (cont.)

Example 39: Pyotr Ilyich
Tchaikovsky, Symphony
no. 2.

War days of large orchestras and larger fur coats, it had been fashionable to indulge in picturesque *Kitsch,* from Rimsky's choreographed *Scheherazade* down to Richard Strauss's *Josephslegende,* Parisian tastes in the '20s veered instead toward the *classique,* in some measure owing to the unwitting initiative taken by Stravinsky's works of that period. It should nonetheless be stressed that this initiative—or rather, what had led it to be taken for such—was not at the root of Stravinsky's absurdly publicized, so-called change of style. Instead, it was the ever-increasing certainty of his continuing exile from Russia that made him, so to speak, turn his own Russian experiences upside down, and this led him henceforth to affirm through his own music, in a cosmopolitan context, what he knew to be the most professional, most accomplished, most ably crafted outgrowths of Russian compositional tradition, and thereby also to deny Rimsky-Korsakov as a reasonably dependable source for any tradition of that sort to spring from. Whereas the music written during his years in Switzerland could still connect Stravinsky to the Russia of his early manhood, and whereas his successes, from 1910 on, could still justify his regarding Tchaikovsky as not altogether relevant to his then current concept of a Russian tradition—a tradition that, after all, Stravinsky could invent on his own, so long as he wrote expressly "Russian" pieces, incorporating folk materials, tales, local instruments, Russian puns, "in" jokes and wordplay, etc.—the music he was to compose as an eventual French citizen, and later as an American by adoption, had to turn away from all that, and needed, rather, to find support—inasmuch as he could not and would not deny his Russian musical background—in a more substantial heritage, through Russia's only thoroughly "Westernized" professional composer to have preceded him. I conclude, therefore, that Stravinsky's decision in this regard was taken in full deliberateness—as was its concurrent ancillary one that was to cause the "neoclassic" tag to be affixed—and that it is in this same sense that he was over thirty years later to turn for encouragement, following Schoenberg's demise, to *that* compositional world, whose rich and varied traditions were so much older.

SONATA FORM IN *Stravinsky*

JOSEPH STRAUS | *Queens College, City University of New York*

No piece of music exists in isolation or can be fully understood apart from its predecessors. But, while no work can entirely avoid referring to the past, some works do so in a more explicit manner than others. There is a whole class of works, such as avant-garde works of this century, that relate to the past primarily by means of negation or denial.[1] For another large class of works, references to the past are explicit but superficial and do not significantly shape the structure of the new work. Frequently in pieces of this type, a traditional form is uneasily grafted onto a fundamentally unrelated musical structure. Milton Babbitt is referring to just this antagonism of form and underlying structure when he speaks of "the merely thematic formalism" resulting from "the transference of the external 'forms' of triadic music to twelve-tone contexts, resulting in a divorce of these 'forms' from their essential tonal motivation."[2]

Another group of works, which alone may properly be called neoclassical, makes conscious, explicit reference to earlier models (most often from the eighteenth century) in such a way that the relationship of the work to its predecessors lies at the aesthetic and structural center of the new work. In such pieces, the reinterpretation of certain explicitly invoked models shapes the musical structure in a profound way. Here is no "merely thematic formalism" but an attempted synthesis of classical forms with modern harmony and voice leading.

It has been generally acknowledged that Stravinsky's invocation of earlier models, and neoclassicism in general, were, to a significant extent, a reaction against perceived Romantic excesses. Stravinsky's disparagement of Wagner for the "murky inanities of the Art-Religion"[3] and the "insult to the dignity" of endless melody[4] are typical of a common distaste in the first part of this century for much of late Romanticism. To aid them in their struggle to resist the influence of their

1. Even as extreme an example as John Cage's 4'33", while obviously avoiding overt reference to earlier music, can be fully appreciated only through knowledge of the norms it denies.

2. Milton Babbitt, "Some Aspects of Twelve Tone Composition," *The Score* 12 (1955):55.

3. Igor Stravinsky, *Poetics of Music,* trans. Knodel and Dahl (Cambridge, Mass.: Harvard University Press, 1947), p. 60.

4. Ibid., p. 62.

immediate predecessors, neoclassical composers made use of forms and procedures from still earlier music, usually from the eighteenth century. By linking their music closely to that of an earlier era, neoclassical composers attempt to circumvent the overwhelming presence of their immediate predecessors.

The relationship between traditional and modern elements—the essential problem of neoclassicism—is perhaps most vividly presented in twentieth-century works in sonata form. The principal form of the symphonies, quartets, and piano sonatas of Mozart, Haydn, and Beethoven, the sonata epitomizes the classical style and, to the twentieth-century mind, seems laden with the tremendous weight and prestige of that style. A composer who employs this form inevitably causes his work to be heard in comparison with the classical masterworks.

But the use of sonata form does more than simply establish the classical style as the appropriate musical context; it imposes specific structural restrictions as well. In the classical era, the sonata form emerged as the expression or embodiment of what Charles Rosen and others call "the polarity of tonic and dominant."[5] The exposition polarizes two contrasting tonal areas, usually the tonic and the dominant; the recapitulation resolves this polarity in favor of the tonic. The relation of tonic to dominant is the central fact of classical tonal relations—the sonata form is, in some sense, simply an outward expression of that fundamental fact.

In the classical era, form is a manifestation of underlying harmonic structure; for modern pieces in sonata form, however, the order is reversed and the form comes first. This poses a problem for those, like Stravinsky himself, who believe that form is fundamentally a manifestation of structural relations. In Stravinsky's words,

> the constituents of [the] material (eg. a theme or a rhythm) must come into a reciprocal relation, which, in music, as in all art, is called form. The great works of art were all imbued with this attribute, a quality of interrelation between constituent parts, interrelation of the building material.[6]

Such a view poses the problem of writing a coherent piece of music in sonata form in the absence of the tonal relations that engendered that form. How can the form emerge from the "interrelation between constituent parts" when the form exists prior to the development of those parts? Is it possible to create a true twentieth-century sonata?

Stravinsky has offered a small number of fascinating musical answers to these questions. Of Stravinsky's entire output since the *Firebird*, only the first movements of the Sonata for Two Pianos, the Symphony in C, and the Octet are unequivocally in sonata form, comprising an exposition with two theme areas, a

5. Charles Rosen, *Sonata Forms* (New York: Norton, 1980), p. 97.

6. Igor Stravinsky, "Avertissement" in *The Dominant* (December 1927), reprinted in Eric Walter White, *Stravinsky: The Composer and His Works* (Berkeley: University of California Press, 1979), pp. 531–32.

development, and a recapitulation. For the central figure in twentieth-century neoclassicism, that may seem a surprisingly small number of pieces. Apparently, Stravinsky generally did allow the form to arise through what he calls "the interrelation of the building material." These three pieces, however, make a fascinating study for two reasons. First, they provide a unique laboratory for studying Stravinsky's harmony and voice leading. Since certain compositional problems are, in a sense, built into the sonata form, Stravinsky's working out of those problems is thrown into sharp relief. Furthermore, our findings about harmony and voice leading here are likely to be applicable to a wide variety of Stravinsky's pieces.

Second, these pieces pose the central problem of neoclassicism—the relation between a work and its predecessors—in a particularly forceful way. In using the sonata form, Stravinsky confronts the classical style in its most powerful and prestigious manifestation, challenging the classical masters on their home ground. Here, Stravinsky attempts to appropriate the sonata form for himself, to wrest it away from traditional tonal relations, to reanimate and recreate it in a new musical context, to, in his own words, "build a new music on eighteenth-century classicism using the constructive principles of that classicism."[7]

7. Igor Stravinsky and Robert Craft, *Conversations with Igor Stravinsky* (Berkeley: University of California Press, 1980), p. 21.

SONATA FOR TWO PIANOS (FIRST MOVEMENT)

While it is beyond the scope of this paper to offer systematic criteria for determining the central pitch class of a given passage, two criteria can be offered here that have extremely broad applicability in Stravinsky's music. First, a pitch class established in the lowest part and reinforced there by metric placement, reiteration, or duration tends to have priority over notes sounding above or around it. Second, in spite of the absence of traditional harmonic relations, 5/3 chords and seventh chords generally function as reinforcement for their lowest-sounding pitch. By both of these criteria, the music of the opening measures of the Sonata for Two Pianos (shown in ex. 1) is centered on F. In the first nine measures of the movement the F sounds in the lowest part for a duration of twenty-two sixteenth notes, longer by far than any other pitch class. In addition, the F generally occurs in metrically stressed positions. Finally, in a number of places (particularly toward the beginning of the passage), the bass-note F is reinforced by either a triad or a seventh chord.

While the music is centered on F, however, it cannot be said to be in F major, since the F is not established by the functional relationship of tonic and dominant. Furthermore, it is not the F-major triad but the pitch class F that is the tonal center here. In a traditional tonal context, eventual motion to the dominant is virtually

Example 1: Igor Stravinsky, Sonata for Two Pianos. Copyright Boosey & Hawkes, 1945. Copyright owners for the world excluding Western Hemisphere and Israel: Schott & Co., Ltd. London. All rights reserved. Used by permission of European American Music Distributors Corporation, sole U.S. agent for Schott & Co., Ltd.

implicit in the initial tonic. No such motion is implicit in the tonal center F here.

The second theme area of the movement, however, does center on C. We are therefore forced to ask, as we would not be in a traditional context, "Why C?" That is, what precisely motivates Stravinsky's choice of C for the second area? One possible explanation is that the choice is fundamentally arbitrary or, to put it another way, that the choice constitutes simply an homage to tradition. In this view, Stravinsky is merely mimicking in a superficial way the most obvious convention of eighteenth-century sonata form—that the second theme area lies harmonically a fifth above the first area—without employing also the more fundamental tonal procedures that traditionally motivated that harmonic motion.

However, before we accuse the Sonata for Two Pianos of lacking organic unity, we must ask whether that is an appropriate criterion by which to judge it. Although the metaphor of a work of art as a unified, living organism has a long history, in music it is now most closely associated with the theories of Heinrich Schenker. Schenker's essay "Organic Structure in Sonata Form" contends, as its title suggests, that the sonata must be an entity of which all the parts are connected at the most profound level.[8] In Schenker's words,

> the concept of sonata form as it has been taught up to now lacks precisely the essential characteristic—that of organic structure. This characteristic is determined solely by the invention of the parts out of the unity of the primary harmony—in other words, by the composing-out of the fundamental line and the bass arpeggiation.[9]

Works that conform to the formal requirements of a sonata but that lack organic structure are, according to Schenker, "stillborn."[10] Speaking of composers who have absorbed only the most superficial features of the sonata, Schenker says they

> strove after melodies and sudden effects, thinking that they could fulfill the demands for an organic formal structure if they only filled their supposed form with melodies and themes. The result was sufficiently deplorable. Instead of organic works of art, they created works whose parts are comparable to raisins placed in dough—even in a baked cake the raisins are clearly distinguishable. The sonata, however, is no cake; it is a tonal mass formed from a unitary material in which the raisins are not distinguishable.[11]

Schenker's critique of nineteenth-century theories of musical structure is devastating and he has, beyond a doubt, revealed the most significant sources of unity and coherence in common-practice music. But can his standards, particularly the standard of organic unity, be meaningfully applied to Stravinsky? Certainly Schenker's use of classical voice leading as a stick with which to beat modern composers can seem a bit beside the point, as in his discussion of Stravinsky's Piano Concerto.[12] Is it possible that even a concept as historically nonspecific as organic coherence might be similarly beside the point for the Sonata for Two Pianos? Is it thus meaningful to require the pitch center of the second area to justify itself as a

8. Heinrich Schenker, "Organic Structure in Sonata Form," trans. Orin Grossman, in *Readings in Schenker Analysis,* ed. Maury Yeston (New Haven: Yale University Press, 1977), pp. 38–53.

9. Heinrich Schenker, *Free Composition (Der freie Satz),* trans. and ed. Ernst Oster (New York: Longman, 1979), p. 39.

10. *Ibid.,* p. 44.

11. *Ibid.,* p. 52.

12. Heinrich Schenker, "Resumption of Urlinie Considerations," from *Das Meisterwerk in der Musik,* vol. 2 (Munich: Drei Masken Verlag, 1926). Translated in Kalib, "Thirteen Essays from the Three Yearbooks 'Das Meisterwerk in der Musik' by Heinrich Schenker: An Annotated Translation," Ph.D. dissertation, Northwestern University, 1973, pp. 212–16.

culmination of what came before? Certainly we would expect this to be the case in a classical sonata where motion to the dominant is so profoundly implied in the establishment of the tonic itself. At the same time, however, we must recognize that organic coherence is by no means a universal attribute of music, or even of Western art music in this century. One does not have to invoke such problematic concepts as "moment form" to observe that much twentieth-century music, in a tradition stemming from Debussy, depends more on juxtaposition of blocks of sound than on development and composing out. If the C is unmotivated in a traditional sense, if it does not appear as the inevitable outgrowth of a musical progression set in motion at the outset of the piece, does that necessarily constitute a musical or aesthetic failing?

The answer will have to depend to a significant degree on the internal construction of the work itself. A work that establishes fragments or moments as its basic constructive units may render irrelevant or anachronistic a standard of organic coherence. A work in sonata form, however, is a different situation. Here, it seems, the form itself imposes certain demands and constraints. If a piece in sonata form is not finally to be perceived as empty, there must be some intimate relationship between the outward aspect (the formal plan) and the inner workings (harmony and voice leading). The sonata form demands, minimally, that there be coherent, directed motion involving some kind of polarization of tonal areas in the exposition that is reconciled in the recapitulation. Without, at the very least, polarization and reconciliation, there can be no true synthesis of form and structure, of traditional and modern elements.

If organic unity is a valid criterion by which to judge Sonata for Two Pianos, then we must return to our question, "Why is the second area in C?" More specifically, we might ask what there is in the first half of the exposition that motivates the motion to C in the second half. One possible answer is contained in the opening measures where, while the lowest part states an F-major triad, the right hand of the second piano simultaneously arpeggiates a C-major triad. The first-piano part in these measures can be construed as stating parts of a dominant-seventh chord on C with the A in the left hand as a passing note. In this way, we might conceive these opening measures as a juxtaposition of an F-major triad in the lowest part with a C dominant-seventh chord above. Thus the C might be said to be embedded in the F-dominated opening sonority. The C is implied here and realized later as the center of the second area.[13]

This is not, however, ultimately a convincing explanation. First, pitch-class C itself is a very weak presence in this passage, both metrically and registrally. Through the first nine measures of the movement it is heard in the bass for a total of

13. For a similar view, see Jonathan Kramer, "Moment Form in Twentieth-Century Music," *Musical Quarterly* 64 (1978): 177–94.

only four sixteenth notes (compared to twenty-two sixteenth notes for the F). Second, only twice in this passage is the C found in a metrically stressed position in any voice. Finally, five-three or seventh chords built above C occur only twice in the entire passage. Despite the occasional appearance of C 5/3 or C^7 formations in the inner voices, the priority of the F is so strongly and unequivocally established by the means discussed earlier as to undermine fatally any sense of pitch-class C as somehow latent in the passage as a potential tone center. If we cannot identify a C-sonority embedded in these opening measures then we must look elsewhere for an answer to our question, "Why does the second area center on C?"

A second possible explanation for the C might be found in the first theme area's preoccupation with the perfect fourth as a harmonic interval. This interval is frequently formed between the outer voices in metrically stressed positions or at the beginnings or ends of phrases. The piece begins with the fourth F–B♭ formed between the outer voices. On the downbeat of measure 3 both voices have moved down a half-step, forming the fourth E–A. The bass then ascends a ninth to arrive back on pitch-class F, harmonized this time with a B♮ in the upper voice (an augmented fourth rather than the original perfect fourth). In measure 9, at the end of the first phrase, the interval G–C is formed between the outer voices. At this point, there is a pause, then a repeat of the initial music which reestablishes the fourth F–B♭.

It could be argued that such prominent treatment of the fourth relates to, and in some sense motivates, the tonal motion to C for the second theme area. The arrival on C is convincing, in this view, because the intervallic distance between C and F, the fourth, has been given such great structural weight in what came before. Actually, this relationship is even more readily apparent in the recapitulation. Here, the first theme comes in C and the second theme in F. In the transposition of the first theme to C, the outer-voice interval becomes the fourth between F and C, as example 2 shows. When the second area comes in F, not only the interval of the fourth but the specific pitches have already been anticipated. To summarize briefly: the large-scale tonal motion of both the exposition and recapitulation seems to involve movement by fourth—the exposition moves from F to C; the recapitulation moves from C to F. In both cases, this motion is prefigured by the intervallic focus on the fourth in the first theme area.

Even in light of this focus on the fourth, however, this remains a static conception of sonata form. There is an association between the pitch level of the second area and the prominent fourth of the first area, but that is not the same as saying that there is directed motion from the first area to the second area. The use of the fourth in the first area makes it possible to go to C; it even makes the arrival on C

Joseph Straus

Example 2: Igor Stravinsky, Sonata for Two Pianos. Copyright Boosey & Hawkes, 1945. Copyright owners for the world excluding Western Hemisphere and Israel: Schott & Co., Ltd. London. All rights reserved. Used by permission of European American Music Distributors Corporation, sole U.S. agent for Schott & Co., Ltd.

sound more natural and convincing than it otherwise might. But it does not direct the motion inexorably toward C; in fact, nothing in the music does that. There is no sense in this piece in which the C is an inevitable outgrowth of the F. The relation between the two theme areas in Sonata for Two Pianos (in both the exposition and recapitulation) is purely associative; they are a fourth apart and the fourth is an important interval in this piece. But the F does not strive toward the C in the exposition and the C does not strive toward the F in the recapitulation. The principal drama of the traditional sonata—polarization and eventual resolution— has thus vanished from the scene. In Stravinsky's exposition, two areas a fourth apart are juxtaposed. In his recapitulation, both areas are transposed so that they are still a fourth apart. There is no polarization in the exposition (merely juxtaposition) and no resolution in the recapitulation (merely rejuxtaposition).

In Sonata for Two Pianos, Stravinsky has not found, nor perhaps did he seek, a true equivalent for the motivating, directing power of tonic and dominant. The internal construction of the piece thus lacks sufficient force to animate the sonata form in which it is cast.

SYMPHONY IN C (FIRST MOVEMENT)

The absence of a strong, motivated polarity in the Sonata for Two Pianos creates an effect of stasis and immobility that wars with expectations aroused by the sonata form. For the sonata form to be truly revived in the post-tonal era, some tonal relationship must be found to play the form-generating role of tonic and dominant. The first movement of Symphony in C contains Stravinsky's most compelling response to this need.

The polarity embodied in this movement is one of two pitch centers, C and E,

148

and of two triads, CEG and EGB. This polarity comes to play the form-generating role of tonic and dominant in the following ways: (1) the exposition expresses tonal opposition; the recapitulation expresses resolution of that opposition; (2) the second area, EGB, is felt as already implicit in the first area, CEG: (3) the form of the movement as a whole is ultimately felt as an inevitable and spontaneous expression of this fundamental relationship.

Harmonic tension between C and E is apparent from the opening motive of the slow introduction to the final chords of the movement. It would be possible to regard the opening motive of the movement, shown in example 3, as implying the tonality of C major. But the absence of an unequivocal harmonization and the considerably greater musical stress on the B than the C suggests that perhaps it is the C that embellishes the B, not vice versa. Cone refers to this as "the tendency of B to act as a dominant rather than as a leading-tone."[14] In other words, the implied harmonic context here might be EGB, not CEG. The ambiguity implicit in this three-note motive evolves into a harmonic polarity powerful enough to generate a sonata form.

In a common-practice sonata form, the eventual motion to the dominant is implicit in the opening music. In Symphony in C, similarly, the eventual motion to EGB is implicit in the first theme, which is shown in example 4. The melody itself, though not devoid of ambiguity, seems to be centered on C. The harmonization, however, does nothing to confirm this interpretation since it consists of only two notes, E and G, which lend as much support to an E-centered interpretation as to a C-centered one. The theme as a whole establishes C as the pitch class of priority, but the E is simultaneously established as a potential countervailing presence. This C-

14. Edward Cone, "The Uses of Convention: Stravinsky and His Models," *Musical Quarterly* 48 (1962):287–99.

Example 3: Igor Stravinsky, Symphony in C. Copyright Schott & Co., Ltd., London, 1948. Copyright renewed 1976. All rights reserved. Used by permission of European American Music Distributors Corporation, sole U.S. agent for Schott & Co., Ltd.

centered area implies E; the rest of the exposition serves to realize that implication.

The bridge to the second theme is in two parts which, following Cone, I will call bridge A (mm. 60–74) and bridge B (mm. 75–94). Both are centered on the pitch D, particularly bridge B, part of which is shown in example 5. The reiterated D's in this passage have the sound of a dominant pedal. In a traditional context, this pedal would be understood as V/V, directing motion toward V for the second theme area. But here, the D leads not to V (G) but to F, the tonal center of the second theme area. The harmonic motion up to and including the second theme is summarized in example 6.

According to the voice-leading logic of this, and many other Stravinsky pieces, the eventual motion toward E is now inevitable. Stravinsky uses here a procedure I have elsewhere called "pattern completion."[15] Through frequent re-

15. Joseph Straus, "A Principle of Voice Leading in the Music of Stravinsky," *Music Theory Spectrum* 4 (1982): 106–24.

Example 6

iteration, a small harmonic unit gets established as a kind of structural norm for a given composition. Incomplete statements of this unit are felt, logically and perceptually, to require completion. In this sense, the music may be directed toward the missing member.

In Symphony in C, the normative unit is a four-note scale segment of the type semitone-tone-tone or its inversion, tone-tone-semitone (prime form: 0135; Forte nomenclature: 4-11). The music leading to the recapitulation, shown in example 7, provides an example of this. Beginning in measure 214, the pitch-class A is isolated from the prevailing E♭-minor harmonies by contour and register. When the instrumentation is drastically reduced beginning at the end of measure 218, the A♮ is taken up by the clarinet which states it repeatedly, most strikingly as a melodic lowpoint. Finally, in measures 223–224, the clarinet carries the A down to E as the recapitulation begins. As the example shows, this descent traverses the notes A, G, F, and E, which constitute the basic unit. The isolated A of measure 215 has thus initiated a descent along the basic unit, the completion of which signals the beginning of the recapitulation. It is interesting to note that pattern completion directs the motion toward E, not C, thus heightening the tonal ambiguity of the first theme.

Turning back to the exposition and to example 6, the notes C, D, and F, corresponding to the first theme, the bridge, and the second theme, are one note shy of forming the normative unit for this piece. The missing note is E. And, the E, in fact, is the ultimate goal of the exposition. The final measures of the exposition, with their strong cadence on E, are shown in example 8. The resulting harmonic structure of the exposition as a whole is shown in example 9.

Let us summarize our findings about the exposition: first, the exposition as a whole expresses a tonal opposition or polarity between C and E; second, the ultimate move toward E is implicit in the first theme, itself centered on C; third, the motion toward E is forcefully directed by means of pattern completion. In each of these aspects, there is a strong analogy to the role of tonic and dominant in the traditional sonata form. The sonata exposition demands some kind of tonal opposition, a demand for which the C–E polarity seems particularly well suited. Conversely, the C–E polarity seems to have found, in a sonata exposition, a natural and compelling formal expression.

The analogy to tonic-dominant relations, however, is not exact. Traditionally, the exposition is tonally open and requires resolution by a balancing second part

151

that closes on the tonic. In Symphony in C, the exposition is also tonally incomplete, but contains two nontonic areas—F, the pitch center of the second theme, and E, the pitch center of the concluding phrase. Therefore, merely transposing the second theme to the tonic in the recapitulation (the traditional procedure) will not suffice to resolve the tension. Something additional must take place.

Let us compare the structure of the exposition with that of the recapitulation.

Example 7: Igor Stravinsky, Symphony in C. Copyright Schott & Co., Ltd., London, 1948. Copyright renewed 1976. All rights reserved. Used by permission of European American Music Distributors Corporation, sole U.S. agent for Schott & Co., Ltd.

Ex. 7 (cont.)

Example 8: Igor Stravinsky, Symphony in C. Copyright Schott & Co., Ltd., London, 1948. Copyright renewed 1976. All rights reserved. Used by permission of European American Music Distributors Corporation, sole U.S. agent for Schott & Co., Ltd.

Example 9

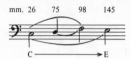

As example 10 shows, the principal alteration in the recapitulation is the displacement of bridge B. In the exposition, it occurs before the second theme; in the recapitulation, it occurs after the second theme and leads to the coda. The fact that this figure is conspicuously missing before the second theme suggests that something might yet be to come, that the tonal issues have not yet been entirely resolved simply by transposing the second theme to C. Just as the polarity of the exposition is not fully set forth until after the second theme, the reconciliation of the polarity in the recapitulation does not take place until the coda.

Example 10

Exposition:	first theme	bridge A	bridge B	second theme	closing theme		
Recapitulation:	first theme	bridge A		second theme		bridge B	coda

The coda does not, however, resolve the polarity in the sense of asserting the priority of one element over the other. Rather, the coda synthesizes the C and E and reintegrates them into a single sonority. In measure 343, the first theme is heard for the final time with, however, a significant modification, as shown in example 11. Instead of asserting C-priority by means of repeated high C's, this modified statement has a sustained high E. This, together with an accompaniment again consisting only of repeated E's and G's, creates a harmonic environment in which neither the C nor the E can be said to have priority.

The same may be said of the final chords of the movement, shown in example 12. These chords have three common tones—E, G, and B—with the E and G retained in the bass. The final chord, consisting of the notes C-E-G-B, has the appearance of a seventh chord on C, but with an E in the bass. The C and the E, polarized in the exposition, are poised together here in a single chord. The central conflict in the movement is thus not resolved in the same way that dominant resolves to tonic; rather, the competing elements are merged and synthesized. Just as the exposition offered a polarity of C and E as a substitute for the traditional polarity of tonic and dominant, so the recapitulation offers synthesis as a substitute for the conventional resolution: polarity and synthesis instead of polarity and resolution.

Example 12

OCTET (FIRST MOVEMENT)

In the first movement of the Octet, Stravinsky has again clearly invoked the traditional sonata-allegro as his formal model. After a slow introduction, the allegro has the customary three sections: an exposition with two contrasting thematic areas, a development, and a recapitulation in which, as in the Sonata for Two Pianos, the first theme comes after the second theme. Example 13 summarizes the formal plan of the movement and also shows the tonal areas involved. The first theme is centered on E♭ and the second theme is a half-step lower, on D. In the recapitulation, the second theme is on E and the first theme is a half-step lower, at its original level of E♭. The tonal motion in both cases is down by half-step,

Example 13

Exposition   Recapitulation

first theme   second theme   second theme   first theme

Eb ⟶ D   E ⟶ Eb

departing from Eb in the first case and descending to Eb in the second.

In sharp contrast to the static juxtapositions of the Sonata for Two Pianos, Stravinsky makes striking use of middleground linear progressions to link the formal sections of the work by means of strong, stepwise voice leading. The motion from the first theme area to the second, corresponding to tonal motion from Eb to D, provides an example of this. The allegro begins with a seven-measure phrase, centered strongly on Eb and cadencing in measure 7. In the eight-measure phrase that follows, the theme is heard in canon with itself. At rehearsal 8, the transition to D and to the second area begins with that most traditional of all transitional devices, the sequence. As example 14 shows, the motion in the upper voice descends by whole step from F# to E to D, the eventual goal tone of the section. Overlapping this arrival on D (at rehearsal 9), other voices begin a new sequential development of the theme starting on a high A and (as the example shows) descending a fifth to D. The arrival on D signals the beginning of the second theme area. I should mention also that in this final linear descent from A to D, the initial A links up registrally to the high Bb which is the third note of the allegro. In this way, the first half of the exposition is powerfully connected to the second half.

For a second example of directed middleground voice leading, let us turn to the music in the recapitulation which connects the second theme back to the first theme. After statements of the second theme on E, imitative entrances of a subordinate melody at rehearsal 19 lead to a cadence on Ab, at rehearsal 20. At this point, where example 15 begins, the upper voice (flute) arpeggiates up to a high Ab, embellishes that tone, then descends stepwise to D, which resolves to Eb to begin the recapitulation of the first theme. Linear descents thus connect the contrasting harmonic areas in both the exposition and in the recapitulation.

Example 14: Igor Stravinsky, Octet for Winds. Copyright 1924 by Edition Russe de Musique; renewed 1952. Copyright and renewal assigned to Boosey & Hawkes, Inc. Revised version copyright 1952 by Boosey & Hawkes, Inc. Renewed 1980. Reprinted by permission of Boosey & Hawkes, Inc.

Ex. 14 (cont.)

Example 15: Igor Stravinsky, Octet for Winds. Copyright 1924 by Edition Russe de Musique; renewed 1952. Copyright and renewal assigned to Boosey & Hawkes, Inc. Revised version copyright 1952 by Boosey & Hawkes, Inc. Renewed 1980. Reprinted by permission of Boosey & Hawkes, Inc.

Through motivic development, thematic relations, and linear progressions at the voice-leading middleground, Stravinsky begins to create an organic sonata form analogous to the traditional one. We have not yet considered, however, the most crucial question of all, that of the work's tonal relations. In discussing the Sonata for Two Pianos, we posed the question "Why C?" of the second theme area but could find no convincing response. In the Octet, we must pose a group of similar questions: Why is the second area in D? Why are the two areas reversed chronologically in the recapitulation? And finally, why is the second area transposed to E in the recapitulation? To these questions, I believe we can find convincing answers.

Let us look again at the tonal scheme of the exposition and recapitulation, shown in example 16. In both cases, as we have observed, the motion descends by half-step, first departing from E♭ and then returning to E♭. Taken as a whole, we have the central tone E♭ embellished by chromatic upper and lower neighbors. As a tonal plan, this bears an interesting relation to those traditional sonatas in which the recapitulation begins on the subdominant so that an exact repeat of the exposition at that level will bring the first theme back in the tonic. In such a case (Mozart, Piano Sonata in C Major, K. 545 is one example), the tonal motion in both exposition and recapitulation rises by fifth, moving first from I to V and then from IV to I. In the case of the Octet, however, the defining interval is a minor second instead of a perfect fifth. The descent by half-step in the recapitulation reflects the same motion in the exposition. Thus, the same motion that brought about harmonic openness in the exposition brings about harmonic closure in the recapitulation.

More important, motion to a pitch from a half-step above and below is the most important middleground motive of the piece, appearing particularly at important cadential situations. Its use as the fundamental structure (shown in example 16) reflects these middleground usages. Let us discuss three of the most important of these.

The beginning of the recapitulation is shown in example 17. The E, tonal center of this passage, is approached from F and E♭, that is, from pitches a half-step above and a half-step below. This approach reflects the form of the background and has the force of a strong arrival.

Example 16

Exposition   Recapitulation
first theme   second theme   second theme first theme

A second moment of crucial structural importance is the return of the first theme in the second half of the recapitulation, shown in example 15. At the end of the linear descent discussed earlier, the E♭ is approached from a half-step above (E) and from a half-step below (D). As in example 17, this double neighbor idea has strong cadential force. And, what is more, the melodic motion at this point nearly recapitulates the background tonal structure of the entire movement. That is, this passage, like the structural background, presents the dyads E♭, D and E, E♭, but in reverse order.

Finally, let us consider the opening measures of the slow introduction to this movement, that is, the opening measures of the Octet as a whole (example 18). The opening B♭ progresses first to B♮ at the end of measure 2, then to A♮ in measure 4, and finally returns to B♭ at the end of measure 4. (I am describing the underlying voice leading here, although the instrumentation very closely reflects this.) The first significant voice-leading gesture of the piece thus consists of the establishment of a tone, its embellishment with chromatic upper and lower neighbors, culminating in the return of the initial tone. The background tonal structure of the sonata-allegro is thus presaged in the opening measures of the slow introduction.

By using the upper-lower neighbor idea to motivate the most significant arrivals in the movement as well as to describe the background tonal structure, Stravinsky has lent the work a remarkable coherence. What is more, this governing concept functions here as a substitute for traditional tonic-dominant relations in giving life to the sonata form. In tonal music, the use of tonic and dominant at the local level to form cadences corresponds to the use of tonic and dominant at the highest level as tonal areas. In the Octet, Stravinsky creates a compelling analogy to this relationship by using the chromatic neighbor idea both at the local level to create a sense of cadential arrival and at the highest level, as the structural background.

In this way, Stravinsky is able to recreate and reanimate the sonata form. Not only has he borrowed the traditional thematic relations and developmental procedures of the sonata but, in the more significant realm of tonal relations, he has found an original and compelling analogy for traditional functional harmony. To put it another way, by using the chromatic-neighbor principle at all levels of structure, Stravinsky has created a musical context for which the sonata seems the most natural formal organization. Stravinsky seems to have invented the sonata form himself as a spontaneous working out of his own harmonic and voice-leading procedures. We know consciously that Stravinsky must have begun with the form and proceeded to find an appropriate harmonic content. But as we hear the piece, the process seems to have been reversed, and the form emerges organically from the musical relations.

CONCLUSION

The harmony and voice leading of the pieces I have discussed are in many ways characteristic of Stravinsky. The pattern completion of Symphony in C, the competition between two tone centers a third apart also in Symphony in C, and the chromatic-neighbor idea of the Octet are also found in a large number of other works. In a more general sense, the concepts of polarity and synthesis, so essential to the sonata form, are central to virtually all of Stravinsky's music. It is this last feature that is brought most sharply into focus by Stravinsky's use of sonata form and explains, at least in part, why Stravinsky used the form.

In addition, these pieces may be considered paradigms of neoclassicism; through them we may hope to understand Stravinsky's relationship to the past and to his musical predecessors. Neoclassicism has generally been regarded as a kind of extended homage to classical music. Composers like Stravinsky, it is believed, turn to the style of the eighteenth century out of reverence for the masters of that era, or at least because they prefer that style to the available alternatives. I believe, however, that there may be a darker side to this process. Without presuming to psycho-analyze Stravinsky and his fellow neoclassicists, I think it is possible to impute to them another emotion toward classical music, namely anger—anger at the continuing tyranny of that music over our concert halls, our standard repertoire, and our musical imagination. Stravinsky, I feel, turned to earlier models as much out of defiance as out of reverence. He uses earlier style elements in order to satirize and mock them, not to perpetuate them. His use of sonata form is thus his supreme act of defiance. What better way to pursue his struggle against his predecessors than to establish dominion over the form that epitomizes their works? By leaving the traditional formal outline intact, Stravinsky makes his triumph over the earlier style all the more evident. His task, then, was to evolve a harmonic language powerful enough to remake the sonata from the inside. In Symphony in C and the Octet, he succeeds in that task and seems to bend the form to his own purposes. That he is able to make the sonata so completely his own in these cases is striking testimony to his enduring strength and power as an artist who has mastered his past.

Stravinsky's "REJOICING DISCOVERY" AND WHAT

IT MEANT: IN DEFENSE OF HIS NOTORIOUS TEXT SETTING

RICHARD TARUSKIN | *Columbia University*

§I

True vocal music is written to a pre-existing text, to a work of artistry, of poetry, capable of inspiring a musician. It is moreover essential that the music faithfully transmit the general mood of the poetical work and that it serve as its beautiful and well-fitting attire. It is essential that in quantity the music correspond to the dimensions of the poem, so that the music does not dangle on it like a gown on a hook, so that the text need not be artificially prolonged by repeating stanzas, verses, or individual words, and so that by such repetitions the artistic and elegant form of the poem be not distorted. It is essential that, in singing, the pronunciation of every word be suitably rendered, and that the phrasing of the text and the observance of its punctuation be correct. Besides that, the rhythm of the music and its meter must be in direct correspondence with the meter of the verse, the length of the musical phrase with the length of the text phrase, and, in fine, that the music in every way blend with the word so as to form with it one indissoluble, organic whole.[1]

1. César Cui, "Neskol'ko slov o sovremennykh opernykh formakh" (1889), in Cui, *Izbrannye stat'i*, ed. I. L. Gusin (Leningrad, 1952), pp. 406–8. Translations from Russian are mine.

So wrote César Cui, then Russia's *doyen* of musical criticism, when Igor Stravinsky was seven years old. Like all such dogmatic pronouncements of Cui's, these are framed as rules dictated by sheer Ciceronian common sense, and yet the author attaches an explicitly programmatic significance to them when he notes that "remarkably, before the present time a majority of composers and of the public did not realize the importance of all of the foregoing and willingly deprived themselves of this powerful force of expression and impression." It was a specifically Russian and a specifically realist aesthetic he was summing up, one that had found its prime exponent in Mussorgsky, and that was exemplified *par excellence* in a style of vocal

162

writing Cui had long ago labeled "melodic recitative"—a kind of infinitely flexible, madrigalian arioso with which anyone who has seen *Boris Godunov* is very familiar. "The most accomplished and inspired scene" in that opera, wrote Cui, was the scene in the inn at the Lithuanian border (act 1, scene 2 in the version of 1874). Here is how he described it:

> The music is so closely, so indissolubly bound with the word that it is as impossible to recall a phrase of text without the corresponding music as it is to recall a phrase of music without the accompanying text. . . . The whole scene is written in so lively, so true and so formally free a fashion, . . . the music and text reinforce one another to such a degree, that the scene makes a far stronger impression with music than without, despite all its lofty purely literary distinction.[2]

Here Cui alludes to the fact that Mussorgsky had set a scene from Pushkin's *Boris Godunov* practically verbatim, and a prose scene at that. He is quick to caution, however, that despite Mussorgsky's success, prose is not an ideal medium for music.

> In music a definite and regular rhythmic continuity is desirable. It augments the force of the impression [the music makes]. Of course, in no case should correctness of declamation be sacrificed to this rhythmic regularity. But if the one can be combined with the other, then all the better. And this is entirely possible given the tonic [i.e., purely accentual] quality of our [Russian] verse, with its regular and monotonous succession of stresses.[3]
>
> A text which contained phrases now long, now short, consisting of a diverse, even fractionated number of verses, would evoke in the music a phrase structure correspondingly devoid of symmetry, which would reflect unfavorably on the absolute value of the music. One should not magnify this disadvantage through a constant rhythmic irregularity. Rhyme is not needed. Short verses with a rich rhyme scheme can often actually impart a rather insipid quality to the music. But regular verses in a beautiful meter are indeed highly desirable. In French verses, on the other hand, rhyme is utterly indispensable. It can, albeit to a limited extent, conceal the unsuitability for music of a syllabic [i.e., numerable] versification. Without rhyme, such verses would ultimately turn into prose.[4]

3. The tonic character of Russian stress is so marked, in fact, that even prose displays a kind of metric evenness, with accented syllables spaced regularly, and unaccented ones arranging themselves in formations of short equal values like *gruppetti* between the accented ones. See my "Handel, Shakespeare and Musorgsky: The Sources and Limits of Russian Musical Realism," in *Studies in the History of Music,* vol. 1 (New York: Broude Bros., 1983), pp. 247–68.

4. Cui, p. 412.

For this reason, along with many others, Cui's paradigm of perfected operatic style was Dargomyzhsky's *Stone Guest,* based, like the inn scene from *Boris,* on a preexisting play by Pushkin, but one cast in elegant iambic pentameters, not prose.[5]

Now the reason for dwelling at such length and in such minuscule and technical detail on the writings and opinions of so apparently insignificant a figure as César Cui, is that the aesthetic canon summarized in his article was passed along to Stravinsky as a catechism and was at first accepted by him uncritically and in toto. Not only was he, as one hardly needs reminding, a pupil and disciple of one of Cui's *kuchkist* brothers-in-arms, but he had been brought up in a family that had exceptionally close ties with Cui himself and with the Russian operatic traditions he represented. Vladimir Stasov, the great kuchkist tribune, dubbed Fyodor Stravinsky the great "realist" of the Russian operatic stage, praised him above all for his powers of truthful declamation, and saw in him the ideal portrayer of Leporello, the basso role in *The Stone Guest*.[6] The elder Stravinsky created the highly realistic role of Skula in Borodin's *Prince Igor,* and sang often in his youth to Mussorgsky's piano accompaniment. Cui seconded Stasov's judgment of Fyodor Stravinsky's artistic qualities in a slew of fine notices.[7] And although—inevitably—heavily barbed, Igor Stravinsky's 1960 memoir of Cui was quite surprisingly revealing. After dismissing the older composer's sterile anti-Wagnerism, his nationalism, and his orientalism with a sneer, he confided that

> Cui did help me to discover Dargomyzhsky, however, and for that I am grateful. *Rusalka* [after Pushkin's mermaid poem] was the popular Dargomyzhsky opera at the time, but Cui considered *The Stone Guest* the better work. His writings drew my attention to the remarkable quality of the recitatives in the latter, and though I do not know what I would think of this music now, it has had an influence on my subsequent operatic thinking.[8]

5. For a detailed description of Dargomyzhsky's opera and its influence, see chapter 5 ("*The Stone Guest* and its Progeny") of my *Opera and Drama in Russia* (Ann Arbor, 1981).

6. "K Iubileiu Stravinskogo" (1900), in V. V. Stasov, *Stat'i o muzyke,* vol. 5a (Moscow, 1980), pp. 260–62. For the jubilee benefit performance that occasioned this tribute (3 January 1901, at which Stravinsky sang Holofernes in Serov's *Judith*), Igor Fyodorovich remembered "being sent to Cui . . . with a special invitation [betokening] my father's wish to pay Cui a mark of attention" (Igor Stravinsky and Robert Craft, *Memories and Commentaries* [Berkeley, 1981], p. 60).

7. Cf. *Izbrannye stat'i,* pp. 309, 403, 442.

8. *Memories and Commentaries*, p. 61. Stravinsky continued, "I do not know whether Cui had heard my *Firebird,* and though I think he was present at the first performances of the *Scherzo Fantastique* and *Fireworks,* I recall no hint of his reactions to these pieces reaching my ears." Some reactions were preserved, however, in Cui's correspondence, especially with his confidante, Maria Semyonovna Kerzina (ca. 1865–1926), a Moscow pianist and founder, with her husband Arkadii Kerzin (1857–1914), of the influential Russian Music Circle, an important bastion of musical conservatism in the early years of the twentieth century. On the *Scherzo Fantastique,* for example, Cui wrote: "It's all the same old pompous mediocrity [*napyshchen-naia bezdarnost'*], absence of music, pursuit of sheer sonority, of orchestral effect, various curious combinations of various instruments, absence of logic, of taste, frequent discord and all the rest. And as a result, the complete conformity of all the modernists with one another, the horrible monotony of their pseudo-music—[producing] either indignation or boredom, depending on one's temperament. But the *gros public,* afraid of the charge of being old fashioned, listens to all this nonsense in holy silence and dares not withhold its applause" (25 January 1909; César Cui, *Izbrannye pis'ma,* ed. I. L. Gusin [Leningrad, 1955], p. 387). If that was his reaction to the *Scherzo,* what could he have made of *The Rite of Spring*? This is what: "The other day Koussevitzky performed 'The Celebration of Spring' [*Prazdnik vesny* (the standard Russian title is *Vesna sviashchennaia*)] by Stravinsky, which has broken all records for cacophony and hideousness. It is a treasure chest into which Stravinsky has lovingly collected all manner of musical filth and refuse. In French I would say, 'M-r Stravinsky est un vendangeur musical.' This 'Celebration' has been booed everywhere abroad, but here it has found applauders—proof that we are ahead of Europe on the path of musical progress" (16 February 1914; *Izbrannye pis'ma,* p. 446).

9. See Vasilii Vasilievich Yastrebtsev, *Moi vospominaniia o N. A. Rimskom-Korsakove,* vol. 2 (Leningrad, 1960), p. 370.

That's putting it mildly. As long as he lived even part time in Russia, Stravinsky's thinking on the text-music relationship was dominated by the melodic-recitative ideal as transmitted not only through Cui's writings, but, of course, through the teaching of Rimsky-Korsakov. He had a particularly formative experience on 4 January 1906, when, in honor of Stasov's eighty-second birthday (it would be his last), Rimsky-Korsakov arranged a performance at his home of the then unpublished and all but unknown setting Mussorgsky had made in 1868 of the first act of Gogol's comedy, *Marriage,* the most uncompromisingly realistic recitative opera ever attempted. Stravinsky's brother Gury was among the performers, and the budding composer, accompanied by his fiancée Catherine (they were married one week later) joined an audience of thirty-five of Saint Petersburg's leading musicians (including Chaliapin and Glazunov) to hear this legendary "experiment in dramatic music in prose."[9] The results of this exposure may be seen in *Le rossignol,* not only in the first act, which was composed before *The Firebird,* but even in the third act, composed as late as 1914. The Chinese Emperor, suffering his death agony against a ritual chorus of unseen spirits (a situation reminiscent of the death of Boris Godunov), sings a passage that could have come straight out of *Marriage* (ex. 1a). Let us in fact compare it with Mussorgsky's opera (ex. 1b). It has all the earmarks of Mussorgsky's special brand of realistic speech-song: careful observation of the intonational contour and tempo of Russian conversational speech, in this case highly agitated, and, above all, extreme care in the handling of the tonic accent. Stressed syllables fall on the beats while the unstressed syllables arrange themselves freely into *gruppetti.* Where words begin with unaccented syllables, the beginnings of beats are occupied with rests, producing a plethora of what Russian writers call "mute endings" (*glukhie okonchaniia*), that is, the interruption by a rest on the beat of a string of short unaccented note values. At the one spot where an accented syllable does fall off the beat (the final "múzyki"), Stravinsky fastidiously marked an accent, even though the high E♭ would hardly be sung without one. Stravinsky was well aware of the source of these prosodic practices. While at work on the first act he wrote in his diary, "Why would I be following Debussy so closely, when the real originator of this operatic style was Mussorgsky?"[10] It is noteworthy, in fact, that there is less of Debussy and more of Mussorgsky in the post-*Rite of Spring* acts of *Le rossignol* than in the pre-*Firebird* one.

10. *Memories and Commentaries,* p. 133.

The same specifically Russian fastidiousness in declamation can be found in the works composed during Stravinsky's brief flirtation with Russian symbolist poetry. Between 1907 and 1911 he set two poems from Sergei Gorodetzky's collection *Iar'* (Saint Petersburg, 1907), and three from Konstantin Balmont's *Zelionyi*

Richard Taruskin

Example 1a: Igor Stravinsky, *Le rossignol,* act 3. Copyright 1941 by Edition Russe de Musique. Copyright assigned to Boosey & Hawkes, Inc., 1962. Reprinted by permission of Boosey & Hawkes, Inc.

Specters: Think back! We are all your deeds. We are here to stay! O think back. Think back on us!

Emperor: What's this? Who are they? I don't know you! I don't want to listen to you! Quick, some music! Music, music! Bring on the big Chinese bass drums! O music, music!

Example 1b: Modest Mussorgsky, *Zhenit'ba (Marriage),* 1868.

Fiokla: You pestered me yourself: find me a wife, old woman, that's all I ask!

Vertograd (Saint Petersburg, 1909). The opening line of The Dove (*Golub*), one of the *Balmont* settings, is a very paradigm of fussily accurate declamation (ex. 2). So as to keep the unaccented last syllable of "k téremu" off the third beat, the word is set as a triplet, voiding the third beat with a typical "mute ending." Even Balmont's

166

mystical *Zvezdoliki* is set in a thoroughly "realistic" fashion as to declamation (ex. 3). The composer's whole effort seems bent on realizing Cui's behest that "in singing, the pronunciation of every word be suitably rendered, and that the phrasing of the text and the observance of its punctuation be correct," even though the text in question is one whose meaning is deliberately veiled, and whose intelligibility is beyond the power of any composer to vouchsafe. "I couldn't tell you even now [!] exactly what the poem means," wrote Stravinsky a half-century after he set it, "but its words are good, and words were what I needed, not meanings."[11] But this was the composer of the *Canticum sacrum* and of *Threni* speaking, not the composer of *Zvezdoliki*. Every aspect of the Balmont setting belies the remark.

11. Ibid., p. 83.

Example 2: Igor Stravinsky, *Two Poems of Balmont* (1911), *Golub* ("The Dove"), first line, with hypothetical version in equal eighths. Copyright by Edition Russe de Musique; copyright assigned to Boosey & Hawkes, Inc. Copyright New arrangement 1956 by Boosey & Hawkes, Inc.

[The dove pressed itself to the tower.]

Example 3: Igor Stravinsky, *Zvezdoliki* (1911), rehearsal 11 to end, chorus parts only. Copyright 1971 renewed by Rob. Forberg–P. Jurgenson. Reprinted by permission of C. F. Peters Corporation, sole selling agents for Rob. Forberg.

[The sky was streaked with red, and seven golden constellations led us to the end of the desert.]

The ultra-refinement of Stravinsky's Russian prosody in this early period, as a matter of fact, provides strong internal evidence that his first ostensible setting of a foreign language, the *Poèmes de Verlaine* of 1910, were composed not to Verlaine's text at all, but to the Russian translation by Stravinsky's close friend Stepan Mitusov. (This will perhaps console certain French critics.)[12] Consider, for example, the setting of the title phrase of "Un grand sommeil noir," which transgresses

12. Cf. Robert Siohan, *Stravinsky* (New York, 1970), p. 32.

13. It is perhaps for this reason that Georgii Ivanov, the compiler of the standard bibliography of settings of Russian poetry (*Russkaia poèziia v otechestvennoi muzyke*, vol. 2 [Moscow, 1969], p. 234) counts the Verlaine songs as Russian and attributes the texts to Mitusov.

French declamation in so many ways at the very outset of the song and also in the setting of "Je perd la mémoire," (ex. 4a) and compare it with the Russian ("Dúshu skováli," literally, "My soul is fettered"), whose tonic stresses it mirrors faithfully (ex. 4b).[13]

Example 4a: Igor Stravinsky, Two Poems and Three Japanese Lyrics, *Un grand sommeil noir* (Poèmes de Verlaine, op. 9 [1910]), French text. Copyright 1956 by Boosey & Hawkes, Inc. Renewed 1984. Reprinted by permission of Boosey & Hawkes, Inc.

Example 4b: Russian text by Stephan Mitusov.

[Gloomy dreams have oppressed my soul: sleep, hopes; sleep, desires. My memory grows weak; I cannot see.]

And now we must confront a great irony, one of the central ironies of Stravinsky's career. For, as one hardly need point out, in the course of the next few years Stravinsky transformed himself into a vocal composer as far from the Cui ideal as it was possible to become. There is not a single precept in the lengthy extract with which we opened our discussion that Stravinsky did not baldly and willfully transgress. The texts he chose were often very far from what is normally considered "artistic." His settings of them were often deliberately and seemingly arbitrarily misaccentuated, distorted as to phrasing and punctuation, dislocated in meter vis-à-vis that of the text, and, in fine (to paraphrase Cui), so calculated as in no way to blend with the word or to permit the formation of "an indissoluble, organic whole." For this, of course, he has been severely chastised, and prosody is perhaps the one aspect of Stravinsky's work that remains today as controversial as it was when his music was new. Most often attacked are Stravinsky's settings of English, a language he spoke poorly, where British and American critics have felt confident that the composer's lapses could be attributed to ineptitude. Yet a study of Stravinsky's Russian text settings in the years of his Swiss exile must decisively put that charge to rest. For every transgression one finds in *The Rake's Progress* or the *Cantata* can also be found in works like *Renard* or *Les noces,* where there can be no question of ineptitude, especially as we have seen how faithfully Stravinsky could set his native language when that was his aim. Any deviations in any language from the prosodic methods already shown should therefore be regarded as intentional.

Our task, then, will be to trace the process of Stravinsky's self-liberation from the Russian prosodic traditions born of realism, to identify the sources of his inspiration and of his methods, and to offer an aesthetic rationale for what amounts to an utter *volte-face*. A tall order, admittedly, for a short paper, but a few provocative points will, I hope, emerge from even a cursory review of the question.

§II

The earliest work in which we find deliberate and conspicuous departures from the norms of correct Russian declamation is the set of Japanese Lyrics composed, to a Russian text by the orientalist A. Brandt, concurrently with *The Rite of Spring*. When Russian musicians received copies of this work following its publication in May of 1913, even the most avant-garde among them were bewildered by the "constant and stubborn disharmony between musical meter and text," as Vladimir Derzhanovsky put it in a letter to the composer.[14] Indeed, a glance at the voice part of *Akahito*, the first song in the set, will show that every tonic stress is quite systematically, and therefore, it seems, perversely, placed on the off-beat (ex. 5a). Nikolai Miaskovsky observed drily in a letter to Prokofiev that these songs "are declaimed with such a delightful regularity that the words could be sung with the correct accentuation by merely moving the whole kit and kaboodle one eighth note to the left."[15] (Cf. ex. 5b, where the song is written out that way.) A sketch page recently published in *Stravinsky in Pictures and Documents* confirms Miaskovsky's half-jocular surmise in the most surprising way: it shows a number of early drafts of the concluding phrases of the voice part, in which not only are the verses set beginning with upbeats (i.e., "one eighth note to the left"), but other conventional prosodic devices, such as the lengthening and the high placement of the climactic word "sneg" (snow), were also originally called into play. Stravinsky, in other

14. July 12, 1913. Vera Stravinsky and Robert Craft, *Stravinsky in Pictures and Documents* (New York, 1978), p. 107. Derzhanovsky was the editor of *Muzyka*, the leading contemporary music forum in Moscow and director of the Moscow organization of the Evenings for Contemporary Music. The translation of this letter in Robert Craft, ed., *Stravinsky: Selected Correspondence*, vol. 1 (New York, 1982), p. 50, is seriously garbled.

15. June 3, 1913. S. S. Prokofiev and N. Ia. Miaskovsky, *Perepiska* (Moscow, 1977), p. 106. The letter is partly translated (but not entirely correctly) in *Stravinsky in Pictures and Documents*, p. 107.

words, initially conceived *Akahito* in his heretofore wonted, conventional, prosodic manner, and then deliberately distorted it (ex. 6).

Stravinsky sent Derzhanovsky an explanation of what he was up to, and Derzhanovsky had it printed in his magazine *Muzyka* in December 1913, as part of the advance publicity for the Russian première. Here is what Stravinsky wrote:

My Japanese romances are composed to authentic Japanese verses of the VIII and IX centuries A.D. (in translation, of course). The translator preserved with precision the exact number of syllables and the distribution of the words in lines. As in the Japanese language, so in Japanese poetry there is no such thing as accentuation. There is quite a lot of interesting information on this matter in the preface to the little book of verses from the Japanese [*Stikhotvoreniia iaponskoi liriki*—hence Stravinsky's original Russian title for the set] from which I drew three verses.

I let myself be guided by these ideas—chiefly the absence of accentuation in Japanese verse—as I composed my romances. But how to achieve this? The most natural course was to shift all the "long" syllables onto musical "short" [beats]. [Stravinsky is using the terms long and short in a conventional way to describe Russian tonic scansion, which is qualitative, not quantitative.] The accents thus ought to disappear of themselves, so as fully to achieve the linear perspective of Japanese declamation.

Example 5a: Igor Stravinsky, Two Poems and Three Japanese Lyrics (1913) *Akahito*, voice part only. Copyright 1956 by Boosey & Hawkes, Inc. Renewed 1984. Reprinted by permission of Boosey & Hawkes, Inc.

Example 5b: The same, "one eighth note to the left."

[I wanted to show you the white flowers in the garden. But the snow fell and you can't tell where there is snow and where there are flowers.]

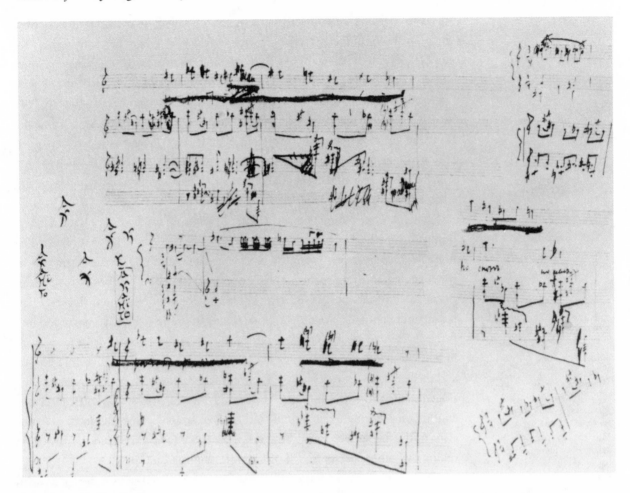

Example 6a: *Akahito*, sketch of the ending (*Stravinsky in Pictures and Documents*, p. 107). Reproduced by permission of the Paul Sacher Foundation.

Example 6b: Transcriptions from same.

Ex. 6b

It would have been a crude error to observe this principle only for the Japanese language, for, in singing these romances in European languages, one would deprive them of what to me is the most precious thing—the unique linear perspective of Japanese declamation.

As to the preposterous impression this declamation supposedly makes, that doesn't embarrass me at all. It is on the level of conventions, which are subject, after all, to the rule of habit.[16]

16. Stravinsky's letter is dated 21 June (O.S.)/4 July 1913; it is quoted here from *Muzyka*, no. 159 (7 December 1913):834–35.

17. *An Autobiography* (New York, 1962), p. 45.

This explanation will serve to amplify the rather inscrutable remarks Stravinsky made about the Lyrics in *Chroniques de ma vie,* where he claimed that "the graphic solution of problems of perspective and space shown by [Japanese painters and engravers] incited me to find something analogous in music," and that he "succeeded by a metrical and rhythmic process too complex to be explained here."[17] The impetus toward creating a "Japanese perspectiveless style" came not from the visual arts directly, but from Brandt (who may well have drawn the analogy in his preface), and not, moreover, until a first draft of *Akahito* had been sketched observing all the rules of conventional Russian declamation according to what Stravinsky, in his letter, called a "crude error" of style.

The idea, to summarize and clarify Stravinsky's somewhat oblique description of his method, had been to capture, despite the use of Russian words that normally carry a strong tonic (dynamic) accent, something of the quality of Japanese numerable versification. What he omitted from his description was perhaps the most significant operative factor: rigorous isochrony. In *Akahito* the voice part is practically limited to one note value, the eighth note, which is, moreover, uniformly present in the movement of the music thanks to the use of a six-note ostinato in the instrumental accompaniment. Thanks to this rigidity of rhythmic motion and the sedulous displacement of the tonic stress onto offbeats, Stravinsky envisioned a situation in which the verbal and musical stresses would cancel one another out, leaving a dynamically uninflected, stressless line, the musical equivalent of the flat surface (what Stravinsky, probably following Brandt, insisted on calling the "linear perspective") of Japanese paintings and prints.

18. Derzhanovsky's letter, dated 24 July 1913, is printed in Robert Craft, ed., *Stravinsky: Selected Correspondence* (New York, Alfred A. Knopf, 1982), 1:51. Miaskovsky's retort (2 July [O.S.] 1913) is in N. Ia. Miaskovsky, *Sobranie materialov,* 2d ed. (Moscow: Muzyka, 1964), 2:362. Miaskovsky had given a more balanced critique a couple of weeks earlier, though still expressed with his typically ironic nonchalance: "Here's what I think about Stravinsky: All this is well and good (his letter I'm returning to you: after all, it's a letter from I. Stravinsky!), Japanese verses are linear and all the rest, but when I played and read his little pieces, I instinctively wanted the whole time to rub my ears and shake my head to get rid of that intrusive horsefly, his willful declamation; but the music itself I like: there is much in it that is personal, "linearly" intimate, harmonically fresh, and Glory be, un-Scriabinish" (20 June 1913: *Sobranie materialov* 2:359).

It was an interesting experiment, but one that violated every canon of Russian taste, and no one bought it. Even Derzhanovsky was at bottom unconvinced. "My guesses," he wrote Stravinsky, "which I was already prepared to employ in defense of the work against the critics' strictures, were confirmed. And yet," he added, "I am somewhat anxious at the thought of that eventuality." Miaskovsky, to whom Derzhanovsky sent Stravinsky's letter, responded with undiminished irony: "after all is said and done, [Stravinsky's] Russo-Japanese declamation is still an absurdity!"[18]

But perhaps there is a simpler way of viewing the Japanese Lyrics within the context of Stravinsky's immediate artistic environment at the time of their creation. As has been pointed out before, these settings, though often factitiously compared with *Pierrot Lunaire,* which Stravinsky heard in Berlin while at work on them, actually represented his closest point of contact with the younger generation of French modernists, whom he met after the premiere of *The Firebird.*[19] The chief stimulus in setting the Japanese Lyrics was evidently Stravinsky's friendship with Maurice Delage, *Akahito*'s dedicatee and the translator of the whole set into French.

19. See Jann Pasler, "Stravinsky and the Apaches," *The Musical Times* 123 no. 6 (June 1982):403–7, especially the last page, where Stravinsky's "abstract" treatment of his text is discussed (though Pasler seems to think Stravinsky set the Lyrics to French—or even Japanese—words directly); also Takashi Funayami, "Three Japanese Lyrics and Japanism," paper delivered at the International Stravinsky Symposium, San Diego, 14 September 1982, at which one of Delage's *Sept Hai Kaï* was performed.

20. The complete continuity draft of "Mazatsumi," the second of the Japanese Lyrics, on pp. 135–38 of the Boosey and Hawkes facsimile publication, *The Rite of Spring: Sketches 1911–1913* (London, 1969) confirms this analysis: the word *zaprýgali* (leapt) (mm. 23–24 in the finished score; p. 136 in the sketchbook) has been deliberately moved a quarter note "to the left" so as to mitigate its tonic stress.

21. Cf. my "Russian Folk Melodies in *The Rite of Spring*," *Journal of the American Musicological Society* 33, no. 3 (1980):501–43.

22. "From *Firebird* to *The Rite*: Folk Elements in Stravinsky's Scores," *Ballet Review* 10, no. 2 (Summer 1982):72–88; also "From Subject to Style: Stravinsky and the Painters," to appear in the proceedings of the International Stravinsky Symposium.

And it was probably the sensitive French prosody of Delage's Hindu songs and haiku settings (at least as much as Japanese prosody, which Stravinsky did not know at first hand but only through Brandt) that provided the model for Stravinsky's declamation. By shifting the words of *Akahito* "one eighth note to the right" (to paraphrase Miaskovsky), Stravinsky sought to neutralize the Russian tonic accent and achieve the "syllabic versification" to which Cui (half French himself) had already drawn attention as being the antithesis of Russian prosody. The use of beams in the voice part (unique to these settings) must have been meant to further this process. To contrast the Japanese Lyrics with the Verlaine songs is thus amusingly instructive: on the one hand we have French declaimed as if Russian (and in fact probably set in Russian), on the other we have Russian declaimed as if French.[20]

As in other ways, so from the declamational point of view the Japanese Lyrics were a cul-de-sac for Stravinsky. His prosodic innovations were contrived: literally imposed in the course of work as an afterthought, not the principled procedure he claimed it was in the *Autobiography* and in his defensive letter to Derzhanovsky. And again, as in other ways, what finally led him out of the blind alley and irrevocably out of bondage to the constricting Russian realism in which he had been brought up, was a new and unprecedented approach to Russian folklore—new and unprecedented not only for Stravinsky but for Russian art music as a whole.[21]

§III

I have attempted elsewhere to account in general cultural and aesthetic terms for Stravinsky's turn to Russian folklore as an unmediated stylistic resource.[22] This "neo-nationalist" trend reached its apex in Stravinsky's work during his period of residence in Switzerland, from 1914 to 1919. During this period he composed two major concerted pieces—*Les noces* and *Renard*—four sets of short solo songs—*Pribaoutki, Berceuses du chat, Trois histoires pour enfants, Quatre chants russes*—and one set of choruses—the so-called *Podbliudnye* or "Saucers"—to folk texts. What attracted Stravinsky in folk poetry was the same thing that had attracted musicians to the symbolists, and something, moreover, that Russian symbolists like Gorodetzky had already long since recognized and appropriated from folk poems: verbal music. Just how important this play of lingual sounds was to Stravinsky at this particular creative juncture may be gauged from the fact that his observations in *Chroniques de ma vie* on what he called the "sequences of words and syllables" in folk poetry, "and the cadence they create, which produces an effect on one's sen-

23. *An Autobiography,* p. 53.

24. See *Expositions and Developments* (Berkeley, 1981), pp. 101–3. The retraction is not convincing, amounting in the end to nothing but an equivocating tautology: "Music expresses itself" (to which, in a filmed interview, Stravinsky once rather quaintly added, "eloquently").

25. This dismantling process had a classic manifestation in 1914: Benois's staging of Rimsky-Korsakov's *Le coq d'or,* in which the singers were confined to the wings and only dancers appeared on stage. This provided a tremendous precedent where Stravinsky was concerned. *Le rossignol, Renard* and *Les noces* were all staged that way, and the latter two were actually composed for such a staging, as was *Pulcinella,* where the song element is utterly disembodied.

26. *Expositions and Developments,* p. 121.

27. Ibid.

28. Bruno Nettl, "Words and Music: English Folk Songs in the United States," in Charles Hamm, Bruno Nettl, and Ronald Byrneside, *Contemporary Music and Music Cultures* (Englewood Cliffs, 1975), p. 198.

sibilities very closely akin to that of music,"[23] was the passage that immediately preceded, and indeed furnished the springboard for the famous diatribe on music and expression, that "over-publicized bit" which Stravinsky would try so hard to live down when it became important to him to forge a link with the expressionist-based music of the Second Viennese School,[24] but which still must be regarded as the linchpin of his postwar modernism. It was precisely the dissociation of sound from meaning (present in all poetry to some degree, of course) that provided Stravinsky with a reassuring validation and a powerful weapon in his avowed aim, if we may put it so, of dismantling the Gesamtkunstwerk.[25]

And where folk poetry went much further in this dissociation even than that of the symbolists (and in directions Stravinsky could never have taken when he was actually setting the symbolists) was in its distensions of stress, something fully revealed only in singing. "One important characteristic of Russian popular verse," Stravinsky recalled forty years after the fact, "is that the accents of the spoken verse are ignored when the verse is sung."[26] This is not quite accurate, since the verses in question are never actually spoken, only sung, and hence are not subject to distortion in quite the way he meant, but merely representative of that distortion. Nonetheless, the differences between sung and spoken accentuation are manifest in Russian folklore, and vastly suggestive to Stravinsky: "The recognition of the musical possibilities inherent in this fact was one of the most rejoicing discoveries of my life; I was like a man who suddenly finds that his finger can be bent from the second joint as well as from the first."[27] Tracing the process of this discovery will show how unexpectedly concrete it was, and how concrete its effects on Stravinsky's music. A few preliminary remarks are perhaps in order.

First, the prosodic distortions encountered in folk singing are a very different matter from the prosodic distortions of the Japanese Lyrics, for the tonic stress is not suppressed, merely shifted. The end product is as authentically and endemically a Russian prosody as the fastidiously realistic speech song of Dargomyzhsky or Cui. But (for a second preliminary) such a phenomenon is by no means restricted to Russian folk song. It is probably a universal trait in the folk singing of tonically stressed languages, like Spanish (as Claudio Spies informs me), or, for that matter, like English. We may be accustomed to assume that Anglo-American folk songs show "a close structural correspondence between words and music," that "at various levels—stanza, line, verse foot, and musical measure—units of words and music correspond closely," and that "stressed syllables are set to musically stressed notes";[28] yet a glance at any field-collected anthology of such songs will turn up many accentual irregularities, as in the following examples from Cecil Sharp, a fastidious collector if ever there was one (ex.7).

Example 7: From Cecil Sharp, *One Hundred English Folksongs* (1916; rpt. 1975). Reprinted by permission of Dover Publications, Inc.

#1: Henry Martin

There were three bro-thers in mer-ry Scot-land,

#3: The Knight and the Shepherd's Daughter

Who should ride by but Knight Wil-liam And he was drunk with wine.

#4: Robin Hood and the Tanner

Bold Ar-der went forth one sum-mer morn-ing,

#6: Lord Bateman

He sail-ed East, he sail-ed West, He sail-ed un-to proud Tur-key. There

he was tak-en and put in pri-son, Un-til his life was quite wea-ry.

#8: Little Sir Hugh

It rains, it rains in mer-ry Lin-coln,

#9: Geordie

It's six pret-ty babes that I have got, The sev-enth lies in my bo-dy;

Out of the first ten songs in Sharp's *One Hundred,* misaccentuations occur in more than half. The one in no. 9 is especially telling, as it was so easily avoidable. The others arise from the forcing of refractory words into an overriding metrical pattern. The frequency, amounting in its paradoxical way to regularity, of this practice is perhaps the reason why Sharp never saw fit to call attention to it in the descriptive commentary to his collection.

As a third preliminary, let us note that Stravinsky was by no means the first Russian composer to observe the misaccentuation of Russian folk texts in singing. It was well known to the kuchkists. Balakirev, who holds a position in Russian folk-song collecting quite comparable to Sharp's in England, faithfully transmitted, in

175

his anthology of 1866, a number of striking instances of shifting accents within a single song, something extremely common in dance songs and ritual songs—the very types that were to furnish Stravinsky with most of his models (ex. 8). Ten years later Rimsky-Korsakov published a version of the first of the songs cited in example 8, and even included it in simplified form as the opening chorus of his opera *May Night* after Gogol (1878). In both versions the accentual shift is maintained without adjustment (ex. 9). This rhythmic quirk remained a permanent fixture in Rimsky's folk choruses, as in the following example from *The Legend of the Invisible City of Kityezh* (1906), an opera every step of whose creation was closely witnessed by Stravinsky (ex. 10).

Example 8a: Mily Balakirev, *Sbornik russkikh narodnykh pesen* (1866), no. 9: "Oh we sowed the millet."

Example 8b: "At daddy's gates" (cf. Tchaikovsky, *1812* Overture).

Example 9a: Nikolay Rimsky-Korsakov, *Sbornik russikh narodnykh pesen* (1877), no. 42: "Oh we sowed the millet."

Example 9b: Nikolay Rimsky-Korsakov, *May Night* (1880), opening chorus.

Example 10: Nikolay Rimsky-Korsakov, *The Legend of The Invisible City of Kityezh* (1904), act 2, chorus of drunkards.

So Stravinsky's "rejoicing discovery" had ample precedent. It was something he had long known, only didn't know he knew it. For until he himself turned seriously to folk texts these shifts of stress had little or no aesthetic significance for him; they were merely among the decorative trappings of the *style russe*, a style advanced musical minds in Russia thought passé.[29] Still, there are aspects to Rimsky-Korsakov's use of folklore and folk song that do have aesthetic resonance in the mature Stravinsky. In the Prologue to Rimsky's *Snegúrochka* (1881), for example, folk choruses are frequently juxtaposed with dialogue, and the same characters participate in both. When singing an "impersonal" folk song they treat the text one way; when singing "personally" they treat it very differently. Stravinsky, for whom the impersonal was all, adopted the former manner, though, as we shall see, far from directly. For he had held folklore very much at arm's length during his period of study with Rimsky-Korsakov. The closest he came to it in those days was in his songs to Gorodetzky's pseudo-folk poems "Spring (The Cloister)" and "A Song of the Dew." The first of these songs seems to contain a characteristic Russian stress shift (ex. 11). But the shift is only seeming; it is actually a sophisticated pun. "Doróga" means road; "dorogá" is a feminine predicative form of the Russian adjective *dorogoi*, "dear." So what looks like a playful Russian stress shift creates a meaningful utterance: "the road (or journey) is dear (precious)." It is a typical symbolist effect and far from the world of folk poetry. Rimsky-Korsakov perceived this clearly when he dismissed Gorodetzky's poem as "decadent, impressionistic lyricism [cast in] an artificially folklike Russian," and declared that he, personally, could not see "what pleasure there could be in setting [such] verses."[30]

More evidence that the freedom of accentuation in Russian folk song was not completely new to Stravinsky in 1914 can be found in the Three Little Songs subtitled "Recollection of My Childhood," which he had composed during the previous summer but which (according to the *Chroniques*) were based on melodies he used to amuse his friends with "in earlier years."[31] In *Expositions and Developments* he claimed that he played them to Rimsky-Korsakov in 1906.[32] They are

29. Cf. Vyacheslav Karatygin's obituary for Balakirev in *Apollon* (1910), no. 10 (quoted in my "From Subject to Style"), in which the future of Russian music is predicated in terms of what the author calls "denationalization."

30. Yastrebtsev, *Vospominaniia*, vol. 2, p. 453. The comment was made on 25 December 1907, at a gathering at which Rimsky's daughter Nadezhda sang the song, along with the *Pastorale*, which latter was dedicated to her.

31. *An Autobiography*, p. 50.

32. *Expositions and Developments*, p. 120n.

Example 11: Igor Stravinsky, "Spring (The Cloister)" op. 6, no. 1 (1907), middle section. Copyright by Boosey & Hawkes, Inc. Reprinted by permission of Boosey & Hawkes, Inc.

[Oh, field, my freedom, oh path thou art so dear.]

trifling pieces, hardly more than jingles. As the voice part to *Sorochen'ka* (The Magpie), the first of the set, shows (ex. 12), the Little Songs are full of accentual distensions; but as the effect is "naïf" and parodistic, the result of imitating childish singsong, and as these songs stand utterly alone among Stravinsky's pre-1914 output, little aesthetic or technical significance need be attached to their scansion.

Example 12: Igor Stravinsky, Three Little Songs (1913), *Sorochen'ka* (The Magpie; "Souvenir de mon enfance," no. 1). Copyright by Boosey & Hawkes, Inc. Reprinted by permission of Boosey & Hawkes, Inc.

[Little magpie, don't leap up into the fir tree. She did, and broke her head.
  Give me some string to tie her head.]

§IV

We can, then, take Stravinsky's word that his rejoicing discovery took place when he said it did (that is, when he began to think seriously about *Les noces*), and that it was fundamentally bound up with his modernist revolt against his old post-kuchkist milieu and with his post-*Rite of Spring* determination to depersonalize his art. What, precisely, led him to it? One of the most potent stimuli came from the work of Evgeniia Linyova, the early twentieth-century musical ethnographer, who was the first in Russia to use the phonograph for field research and whose prefaces to her published transcriptions were musically detailed and authoritative to a hitherto unprecedented degree. If Balakirev was the Russian Cecil Sharp, Linyova was the Russian Bartók. Her work was well known to Stravinsky,[33] and, as I have

33. Cf. his letter to his mother (10/23 February 1916) in which he informs her that he has volume 1 of Linyova's transcriptions and asks whether there have been any other volumes issued (L. S. Diachkova, ed., *I. F. Stravinskii: Stat'i i materialy* [Moscow, 1973], p. 488).

34. Evgeniia Linyova, *Velikorusskie pesni v narodnoi garmonizatsii*, vol. 1 (Saint Petersburg, 1904), p. xvi. Stravinsky would have found ample confirmation of these remarks in the collection of wedding songs by Kireevsky on which he drew for *Les noces* (V. F. Miller and M. N. Speransky, eds., *Pesni sobrannye P. V. Kireevskim, Novaia seriia*, vol. 1 (*Pesni obriadnye*) [Moscow, 1911]). Here are a few examples of displacement as Kireevsky noted them down as early as the 1830s:

#183:
Zhurila, govórila,
Govoríla, sama plakala

#192:
Boiarý-li vy, boiáry!

#742:
Vesélaia sem'ia veseláia.

#918:
Iasna sókola vo chistóm póle,
Vo chístom pole vo zelenom,
Sazhala ego na belú rúku,
Prinosila ko rodnoi matushke:
"Matushka moia, gosudarynia!
Izlovila ia iasna sokolá!"
Uzh kak tot-li sokól,
Uzh kak tot-li iasion,
Ty, Seluian gospodin,
Seluian, sudar' Fedotovich!

In the last example, every one of the syllables of the word *sókola* (hawk) receives a stress at some point, and the metrical count is in constant flux.

tried to show elsewhere, uncommonly suggestive to his neo-nationalist creative attitudes.

Linyova was the first Russian ethnographer to make explicit observations on the unusual rhythmic and prosodic traits earlier students of Russian folklore had taken for granted. In the following lengthy extract she touches not only upon the mutability of accent, but also on the metrical irregularities peasant singers habitually introduced into the songs they sang, often—unlike the kinds of distensions we have so far observed, e.g., in Cecil Sharp—decidedly at variance with the prevailing poetic meter.

> From the rhythmic point of view folk song has a property which especially hampers its transcription into fixed notation. This property is the freedom with which accent is displaced in word and verse. The accent in folk song moves from one syllable to another within a word and from one word to another within a verse, according to the demands of the sense of the verse or of the melody, which are closely bound together and mutually influential. In this mobility of accent one feels the urge to destroy monotony, for example: *lúchina, luchína, luchiná* [*recte: luchína*, a torch], or *góry, gorý* [*recte: góry*, mountains]. As a result of this mobility and mutability of [what we may call] the *logical* accent of folk song, it is often very difficult to reconcile it [that is, the logical accent] with the *metrical* accent of contemporary art music (as marked by bar lines), *which strives for mechanical regularity in the counting of time units*. When taking a song down by hand little rhythmic compromises are possible—one can steal an eighth note here, a quarter note there, and in this way smooth over the apparent rough spots and bring the recalcitrant, capricious tune into conformity with a general mold. But . . . the phonograph insistently claims its due and will not admit such errors.[34]

Linyova goes on to pinpoint two very specific characteristics of Russian folk verse, both of which became characteristics, too, of Stravinsky's Swiss-period music.

(i) The number of syllables in the respective hemistichs of a folk verse is not equal. On the contrary, the inequality of the number of syllables in the hemistichs, each of which has one *chief* accent, is one of the characteristic traits of folk song.

(ii) The accent in the verse of a folk song is not *tonic* (that is, mechanically regular, falling on a certain syllable of the verse), but *logical*

Richard Taruskin

[*logicheskoe*], mutable (only occasionally changing position according to the demands of sense, but nonetheless in no way arbitrary). Therefore, although *in general* any song, even the rhythmically most wayward, can be divided into measures, nonetheless, owing to the changing position of the accent and the insertion of one, two or even three syllables into one strain or another (depending on the sense, or simply on the individual inclination of the singer toward exclamations—*èkh, ai no, pravo, da vot,* and so on), one will frequently encounter departures from the division (i.e., the meter) one has adopted.[35]

As she relates, Linyova briefly considered adopting the transcription method developed by the Ukranian composer and folklorist Pyotr Sokalsky (1832–87) in his posthumously published collection (1903) and his important theoretical monograph on Great-Russian and Little-Russian folk music.[36] This method involved abandoning all attempt at metrical barring, using bar lines only to mark the major divisions of the verses (the hemistichs). She decided against this, however, in that in practice it obscured the rhythmic structure of the music. She preferred a system of irregular barring that placed all "chief accents," as she called them, on downbeats.[37] We shall observe this practice in Stravinsky's settings, too.

Once again we should note that the early kuchkists, armed with sharp ears and open minds, had anticipated the scientific ethnographers of the next generation. Balakirev's anthology contains notable instances of Linyova-like irregular barring, including one (song no. 17) that instinctively adopts Sokalsky's hemistich method (ex. 13). And in Rimsky-Korsakov's anthology there is a wedding song that looks as if Stravinsky had composed it (ex. 14).[38]

Alongside Linyova there is another important source to be identified before looking at the impact of Stravinsky's rejoicing discovery on his music—a source even more specifically and directly related to Stravinsky's work. Among the books Stravinsky brought back with him from his last trip to Russia in July 1914—a trip

35. Ibid., p. xvii.

36. *Russkaia narodnaia muzyka, velikorusskaia i malo-russkaia, v eë stroenii melo-dicheskom i ritmicheskom i otlichiia eë ot osnov sovremennoi garmonicheskoi muzyki* (Kharkov, 1888).

37. Linyova, pp. xvi–xvii.

38. In his autobiography, Rimsky-Korsakov recalled of this particular item, "once, at Borodin's, I struggled till late at night trying to reproduce a wedding song [*Zvon Kolokol,* Ringing Bell], rhythmically it was unusually freakish, though it flowed naturally from the mouth of Borodin's maid, Doonyasha Vinogradova, a native of one of the governments along the Volga" (*My Musical Life,* trans. Judah A. Joffe [London, 1974], p. 165).

Example 13: Mily Balakirev, *Sbornik russkikh narodnykh pesen* (1866), no. 17, *Na Ivanushke chapan.*

Na I- vá- nu- shke cha- pán   Chort po mé- sia- tsu ta- skál.

Slý- shish'- li- ty, I- vá- nu- shka, vé- rish'- li, leg- ká nó- zhen'-ka?

(Cf. Sokalsky, barring by hemistichs)

Example 14: Nikolay Rimsky-Korsakov, *Sbornik*, no. 72: wedding song, "The bells are ringing in Yevlashev village."

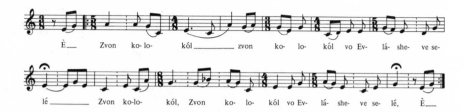

È— Zvon ko-lo- kól — zvon ko- lo- kól vo Ev- lá- she- ve se- lé — Zvon ko-lo- kól, Zvon ko- lo- kól vo Ev- lá- she- ve se- lé, È—

expressly motivated, as is well known, by the need for folk texts for *Les noces*—was one that came not from the Kiev bookseller who had furnished him with his copy of Kireevsky's wedding songs, but from his own father's huge, indeed famous, library. This was Ivan Sakharov's *Skazaniia russkogo naroda* (Legends of the Russian People [Saint Petersburg, 1838]), an enormous miscellany that is occasionally mentioned in connection with *Les noces*[39] but that was actually the source of the texts for the Peasant Choruses (*Podbliudnye*) of 1914–17.[40] Like most of the early Russian folklorists, Sakharov published only the texts of his songs, not the melodies. But in the case of the *podbliudnye,* he felt constrained to comment obliquely on the tunes, precisely because of the way the texts were distorted in singing. His comments were quite ambiguous; it would be difficult to figure out exactly what he was driving at in the extract that follows without our knowledge of Balakirev, Rimsky-Korsakov, and especially Linyova.

The Russian yuletide songs we call *podbliudnye* or *igral'nye,* from their adaptation to games (*igry*), or *obriadnye* [from *obriad,* ritual], belong without out doubt to very remote times which we have no factual basis for deter-

39. Cf. Robert Craft, *Prejudices in Disguise* (New York, 1974), p. 248; later in *Stravinsky in Pictures and Documents,* p. 132. Also Eric Walter White, *Stravinsky: The Composer and His Works* (Berkeley, 1966), p. 33. In both cases, however, the bibliographical citations are faulty.

40. Stravinsky forgetfully gave trusty old Afanasiev (the source of the *Pribaoutki, Renard* and *Histoire du soldat*) as the source of these texts as well (*Expositions and Developments,* p. 119), and he has been followed by all subsequent writers and bibliographers, including White (p. 209) and Dominique-René de Lerma (*Igor Federovitch Stravinsky: A Practical Guide to Publications of His Music* [Kent, Ohio, 1974], p. 78). Craft cited not the familiar Afanasiev *skazki* collection, but his lesser known *Poèticheskie vozzreniia slavian na prirodu* (The Slavs' Poetic Attitudes toward Nature, vol. 2 [Moscow, 1869], p. 194) as the source for these texts (*Stravinsky in Pictures and Documents,* p. 604), but what is actually found there is only a description of the divination ceremonies for which these texts were appropriate—together with a footnote reference to Sakharov! The most famous of the four *podbliudnye* texts—*Shchuka* (The Pike), the third in Stravinsky's set—can in fact be found in this Afanasiev volume (p. 158) as well as in Tereshchenko's *Byt russkogo naroda* (vol. 7 [Saint Petersburg, 1848], p. 158), which was also in the elder Stravinsky's library. Both *Shchuka* and *U Spasa v Chigasakh* (At the Savior's Church in Chigasy, the first of the set) can be found in the 1911 Kireevsky publication (nos. 1059 and 1063 respectively). But Sakharov contains all four texts (3d ed. [1841], vol. 3, pp. 11, 12, 13, 260), and it is the unique source of Stravinsky's nos. 2 and 4.

mining exactly. As creations of folklore, these songs carry a peculiar imprint in the form of a tune which differs from all other kinds in its slow, regular and economical [Sakharov evidently means syllabic] disposition in tones.

Russian yuletide songs come in the following meters: anapestic, dactylochoric with tribrachic endings, choric, dactylic, iambic. Or else they are made up of anapestopyrrhic feet. Lines are found with two, three or four feet. Here are examples.[41]

41. Ivan Sakharov, *Skazaniia russkogo naroda* (3d ed., 1841), vol. 3, p. 10.

And what is the very first example? None other than The Pike (*Shchuka*), the third of Stravinsky's set of choruses, but the first to have been composed. It was completed before the year 1914 was out, and the conclusion seems inescapable that it was Sakharov's prosodic analysis that piqued the composer's interest in setting the text. Look now at example 15 and behold Stravinsky's "rejoicing discovery."

Example 15: Ivan Sakharov, *Skazaniia russkogo naroda* (1841), vol. III p. 10.

РУССКІЯ СВЯТОЧНЫЯ ПѢСНИ БЫВАЮТЪ: АНА-
ПЕСТИЧЕСКІЯ, ДАКТИЛОХОРЕИЧЕ-
СКІЯ, СЪ ОКОНЧАНІЕМЪ ТРИБРА-
ХИЧЕСКИМЪ, ХОРЕИЧЕСКИМЪ, ДАКТИ-
ЧЕСКИМЪ, ЯМВИЧЕСКИМЪ; ИЛИ СОСТОЯТЪ:
ИЗЪ АНАПЕСТОПИРРИХІЕВЪ. РАЗМѢРЪ СТИ-
ХОВЪ БЫВАЕТЪ: ДВУХСТОПНЫЙ, ТРЕХСТОП-
НЫЙ, ЧЕТЫРЕХСТОПНЫЙ. ВОТЪ ПРИМѢРЫ:

ЩУКА ШЛА | ИЗЪ НОВА | ГОРОДА.
ОНА ХВОСТЪ | ВОЛОКЛА | ИЗЪ БѢЛА-
ОЗЕРА.

КАКЪ НА ЩУ | КѢ ЧЕШУЙ | КА СЕРЕБРЯНАЯ.
ЗДѢСЬ ТРЕХСТОПНЫЙ АНАПЕСТИЧЕСКІЙ СТИХЪ
ИМѢЕТЪ ТРИБРАХИЧЕСКОЕ ОКОНЧАНІЕ.

What Sakharov had sought in his pedantic way to prove was that The Pike was sung in "anapestic trimeters with tribrachic endings." What he actually proved is what is by now a familiar story: that the musical ictus distorted the natural accentuation of the poem. Most telling is the fact that the second syllable of the word "Novagóroda," which is merely an infix stemming from the archaic genitive declension of the name of the old Russian city of Novgorod, falls on an accented note in the melody. If read, rather than sung, the three lines given by Sakharov would be accented as follows:

> Shchúka shlá iz Novagóroda. (Slava!)
> Oná khvóst voloklá iz Bela-ózera. (Slava!)
> Kák na shchúke cheshúika serébriannaia. (Slava!)

> The pike came from Novgorod.
> Its tail it dragged from Belo-ozero.
> How silver were its scales!

For a conventionally declaimed setting of the poeticized form of the name Novgorod, compare the opening chorus from Rimsky-Korsakov's opera *Sadko* (1897) (ex. 16).

Example 16: Nikolay Rimsky-Korsakov, *Sadko* (1897), opening chorus.

V No- ve- gó- ro- de ve- lí- kom u nas vsiák se- bé sám, (*etc.*)

[In great Novgorod everyone is his own boss.]

So how does Stravinsky's setting relate to Sakharov's scansion? If one looks at the so-called original version of the chorus (1914), one is apt to be disappointed (ex. 17a). Not only is the second syllable of *Novagóroda* apparently unaccented and thereby conventionalized, but the final syllable (a mere genitive case ending) is set to a long note, spoiling Sakharov's "tribrachic ending."

But now compare the 1954 version of the chorus, with the four horn parts (omitted in the example) (ex. 17b). Amazingly, we now have a perfect transcription of Sakharov's scansion by means of Linyova's method: the bars are so arranged that the accented notes (including the telltale *-a-* of *Novagóroda*) fall on downbeats, and the "tribrachic endings" are set as staccato eighth notes. What is truly paradoxical is

Example 17a: Igor Stravinsky, *Podbliudnye,* no. 3: *Shchuka* (1914), top voice only. Reproduced by kind permission of the copyright owners, J & W Chester/Edition Wilhelm Hansen, London, Ltd.

Example 17b: Igor Stravinsky, Four Russian Peasant Songs (new version, 1954), no. 3: "The Pike." Reproduced by kind permission of the copyright owners, J & W Chester/Edition Wilhelm Hansen, London, Ltd.

that this version, which fits the quirky Russian text so well, was published only with an English text, whose relationship to the new barring is utterly meaningless. It is inconceivable that Stravinsky went back to Sakharov, whom he had apparently forgotten all about (as we deduce from the mistaken attribution of the *Podbliudnye* texts to Afanasiev in *Expositions and Developments*), only to adopt his scansion for an English translation. No, the only reasonable explanation is that the 1954 English-language version actually represents the original Russian conception, and the original publication (delayed until 1930, and brought out by Schott) was misguidedly rebarred (whether by Stravinsky himself or by an editor) either for the sake of simplicity or in order to accommodate the German translation (for no one could have expected Russian performances in the west in 1930). Confirmation of this hypothesis will of course have to come from the still inaccessible sketch material in the composer's archive.

§v

But any doubts as to the importance of Sakharov's example in the formation of Stravinsky's habits of Russian prosody must vanish when one examines the sketches for the first settings he made under its influence—the *Pribaútki* of 1914. Fortunately, a sample page of sketches for the third of them—*Polkovnik* (The Colonel)—has been published, and there we may see how Stravinsky turned Sakharov's analytical method, via Linyova's transcription method, into a compositional tool.

More than any other type of folk text, *pribaútki* represent the kind of pure "mouth music" that was Stravinsky's post-1914 ideal. No wonder they were the first texts (besides *Shchuka*) he set after making his rejoicing discovery: the set was completed within three months of the book-buying excursion to Kiev. The source for them was the very last section, a kind of appendix to Afanasiev's monumental *Russian Folk Tales* (*Russkie narodne skazki*), in which a garland of twenty-three *pribaútki* were collected and set forth not as verse but as prose. And what are *pribaútki*? They are essentially nonsense jingles, often sung either by or to children. The standard musical term for them is *potéshki*. Stravinsky called them *pribaútki* because that is what Afanasiev called them, though the latter term is more generally applied to witty patter of any kind. In a couple of his conversation books Stravinsky made some observations about the genre, but they are faulty and misleading (and absolutely outrageous as to etymology).[42] A far better starting point for an understanding of *pribaútki* can be found in Afanasiev's own commentary. "*Pribaútki*," he observed, "in the form in which one hears them now on the lips of the people, apparently comprise excerpts from a variety of folk verbal prototypes: the songs, stories and [even] the laments which accompany [popular] games and rituals."[43] While not exactly verse, they are nonetheless distinguished, according to the collector, by their strongly rhythmic character, and their heavy use both of rhyme and of alliteration. Rhythm, rhyme, and alliteration, in fact, are far more important in *pribaútki* than meaning. There couldn't be a better example than the third song in Stravinsky's set, a perfect Russian analogue to our own tongue twister "Peter Piper picked a peck of pickled peppers." It is not about a colonel, not about a quail. It is about the letter *p* and (in the second half) about subtly differing rhythmic groups that all end in the vowel *a* (or to be more precise, a schwa):

42. See *Conversations with Igor Stravinsky* (Berkeley, 1980), p. 35; also *Expositions and Developments*, p. 121: "The word *pribaoutki* denotes a form of popular Russian verse, the nearest English parallel to which is the limerick. It means 'a telling,' 'pri' being the Latin 'pre' and 'baout' deriving from the Old Russian infinitive 'to say.' *Pribaoutki* are always short—not more than four lines usually. According to popular tradition they derive from a type of game in which someone says a word, which someone else then adds to, and which third and fourth persons develop, and so on, with utmost speed." Practically none of this is true.

43. A. S. Gruzinsky, ed., *Russkie narodnye skazki A. N. Afanasieva* (Moscow, 1913), vol. 5, p. 240.

Poshól polkóvnik poguliát',	A colonel went a-walking,
poimál ptíchku-perepiólochku;	he caught a little bird, a quail.
ptíchka perepiólochka	The little quail
pít' pokhotéla,	became thirsty.
podnialás'-poletéla,	She rose up and flew away,
pála-propála,	she fell to earth and disappeared,
pod lióð popála,	under the ice she landed.

popá poimála,   She caught a priest,

popá popóvicha,   a priest and son of a priest

Petrá Petróvicha.[44]   named Peter son of Peter.

44. Ibid., p. 238.

I have set the *pribaútka* out not in prose, the way Afanasiev printed it, but with each clause as a line in itself approximating verse, the way Stravinsky did in his sketch book. Turning now to the sketch (ex. 18), what do we find? We find Sakharov's scansion marks set next to each line, and above the "poem" three musical drafts (the two-line sketch at the top of the sheet is for the oboe-clarinet duet at the end of the first *pribaútka, Kornilo*). The two pitched sketches are both for the ending of the song, and both differ considerably from the final version. In the first, the grammatical case is changed for some reason from the genitive to the dative, suggesting that at first Stravinsky may have intended to paraphrase Afanasiev's text rather than set it as it stood (ex. 19a). The most important way in which this sketch differs from the final version is prosodic. Stravinsky at first distinguished the accented syllables from the unaccented ones by lengthening them: they are set either as quarters or as groups of two slurred eighths.

In the second draft of the ending, Afanasiev's text is set without departure, and the melodic figure corresponds to one that is found in the finished song, though not at these words (ex. 19b). Accented syllables are still lengthened here. Now the most revealing sketch by far is the one that has obviously been added as an after-thought, and most likely after the poem had been copied out and scanned at the bottom of the page. It is a purely declamational sketch, showing no pitches, just durations and barrings (ex. 19c). Here Stravinsky hit upon the method he was to employ in the end for the whole song, and in many other settings as well: with only a single exception every syllable in the setting carries the same duration—an eighth note (or, occasionally, a pair of slurred sixteenths)—and accentuation is achieved solely by means of what Linyova called the "logical stress."

In example 20, which shows the whole voice part as Stravinsky finally barred it, and also shows the scansion marks from the sketch, we may finally observe in full the results of his rejoicing discovery. First of all, note that the bracketed section, which corresponds to the third sketch, maintains its declamation exactly (and is set to a single pitch, as the sketch already implied). Second, note that the ending is adjusted to take the stress off the last note: some old Russian prosodic habits of Stravinsky's died a hard death, after all. But lest we be misled into thinking that Stravinsky was still trying to please César Cui, consider the words *podnialás'–poletéla* at the end of the second line, where, as Stravinsky put it, "the accents of the spoken verse are ignored when the verse is sung," that is, where a purely musical

Example 18: Igor Stravinsky, Sketch for *Pribaútki*, no. 3 (*Polkovnik*) (*Stravinsky in Pictures and Documents*, p. 131). Reproduced by permission of the Paul Sacher Foundation.

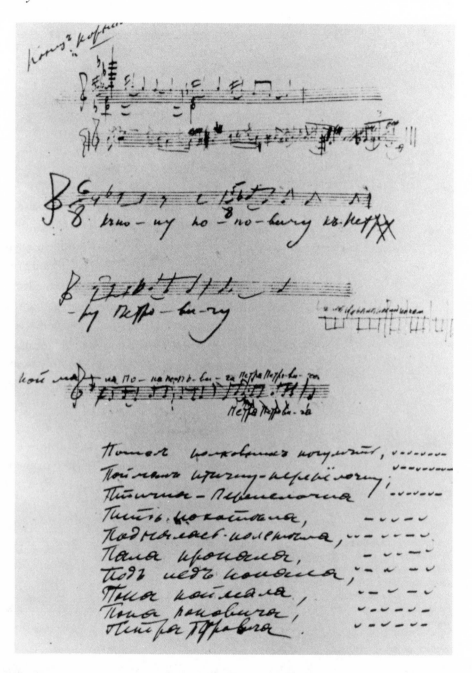

Example 19a: Transcriptions from same.

k po- pú po- pó- vi- chu k Pet- rú Pet- ró- vi- chu

Example 19b,c: Transcription from same.

Ex. 19b

poima- la Po- pá Po- pó- vi- cha Pe- trá Pet-ró- vi- cha

Ex. 19c

Pa- la pro- pa- la pod liod po- pa- la [po- pa poi- ma- la, *etc.*]

sequence is allowed precedence over the verbal accent. And now look at the "sprung rhythm" at the words *poimál ptíchku* in the first line, where the unique succession of two stressed syllables is overridden, again, for purely musical reasons.

The opening of the song is willful to the point of being a bit enigmatic. What is the role of the accents, which never return? Evidently they are meant to countermand the tonic stress on the second syllable (perhaps a carry-over from the "Russo-Japanese" declamation Stravinsky had toyed with a year earlier) and turn the whole measure into an upbeat. There being no readily available sign for the suppression of a stress, Stravinsky seems to have intended to surround the natural stress with ersatz stresses and, by thus equalizing the stress, in effect neutralize the stress.

But the tonic stress remains very much in force, even when honored in the breach rather than in the observance. Stravinsky's post-1914 prosody remained profoundly authentic in its Russianness, only now it was a different Russian tradition to which he pledged allegiance. As in so many other ways, Stravinsky played

Example 20: Igor Stravinsky, *Pribaútki* (1914), no. 3 (*Polkovnik*): voice part only, incorporating the scansion marks from the sketch. Reproduced by kind permission of the copyright owners, J & W Chester/Edition Wilhelm Hansen, London, Ltd.

Po- shól pol- kóv- nik po- gu- liát', Poi-mal ptích-ku pe- re- pió- loch- ku;

Ptích- ka pe- re- pió- loch-ka Pit' po-kho- té- la, Pod- nia lás'- po- le- té- la,

cf. Ex. 19c — Doppio movimento

Pá- la pro- pá- la, Pod liód po- pá- la, Po- pá poi- má- la, Po-

-pá po- pó- vi- cha, Pe- trá Pe-tró-vich-a.

the Russian folk-music tradition against the art-music tradition and used it as his passport to freedom from the academic post-realist milieu in which he had been brought up.

§VI

Now that we have reached the crucial year 1914, we had better stop going piece by piece, for to tackle the major works of the Swiss years would take us far beyond the scope of a modest paper. Still, I do wish to demonstrate that the discoveries Stravinsky made in Sakharov and Linyova were no cul-de-sac, like his Japanese experiments, but a permanently transforming acquisition, and that the attitudes and even the techniques he was on the threshold of formulating stayed with him long after the close of his so-called Russian period, that is, long after he stopped setting Russian texts.

As it happens, the shaping of the prosody in the third of the *Berceuses du chat*—which we can follow in detail thanks to its fortuitous inclusion in the published *Rite of Spring* sketchbook—gives just such a suggestion. The text comes from the section containing lullabies in the same Kireevsky volume whose wedding songs furnished the text for *Les noces*. Again there is a close English analogy: "Hush Little Baby, Don't Say a Word." Kireevsky's text runs as follows:

> Báiushki-baiú, pribaiúkivaiu . . .
> Kach', kach', priveziót otéts kalách,
> Máteri sáiku, sýn[k]u balaláiku,
> A baiú, baiú pribaiúkivaiu . . .
> Stánu ia kacháti,
> V balaláichku igráti,
> A baiú, baiú, pribaiúkivati . . .[45]

> Hushabye, hushabye I sing . . .
> Rockabye, rockabye, Daddy will bring you a biscuit,
> He'll bring Mommy a roll, he'll bring sonny a balalaika,
> Hushabye, hushabye I sing . . .
> While I rock you,
> I shall play the balalaika,
> While hushabye, hushabye I sing . . .

The refrain is what I wish to focus upon. Apparently, Stravinsky first sketched it in a way that respects its accentuation as indicated above (ex. 21a). But he

45. *Pesni, sobriannye P. V. Kireevskim, Novaia seriia* (Moscow, 1911), no. 1108.

189

immediately began to tease it, apparently with the object of exploiting a musical correspondence between the accented "-baiú" and the unaccented "-vaiu." It is difficult to decide in just what order the sketches for this song were made. But if we assume that they made a progressive approach to the version that was published, then the order is as follows: example 21b, which was immediately changed to example 21c, and then to example 21d (these being layers of a single sketch), then to example 21e, and finally to example 21f before ultimately assuming the published form: example 21g.

Example 21a

Example 21b: (p. 110)

Example 21c

Example 21d

Example 21e: (p. 112)

Example 21f: (p. 113)

Example 21g: (from the published score) Reproduced by kind permission of the copyright owners, J & W Chester/Edition Wilhelm Hansen, London, Ltd.

Bá- iu-shki ba- iú, pri- ba- iú- ki- va- iu...

The accentuation of the word *pribaiúkivaiu* is utterly distorted. An argument could be made that *pri-* carries an accent (since it occupies the downbeat), or that *-va-* carries an accent (since it is given an *acciaccatura*), or even that the final *-iu* carries an accent (since it is syncopated and lengthened, like the "sprung" *-ba-* in the first measure). But the third syllable cannot by any stretch be said to carry one. Now to anyone who knows the later Stravinsky, this inside-out setting of *pribaiúkivaiu* will have a familiar ring. The resemblance to "Laudate Dominum" in the Symphony of Psalms is uncanny—right down to the syncopated and lengthened, yet unaccented, final syllable (ex. 22). The shifting stress of the two "laudate's" comes straight out of Kireevsky and Linyova. (The fact that the original words may have been "Góspodi pomílui" does not alter the situation, for Stravinsky saw fit to make no adjustments when substituting the Latin text.) And in turn are we not legitimately reminded of a piece that might fairly have been expected to be the very last Stravinsky composition to figure in the present discussion? (See example 23.)

Example 22: Igor Stravinsky, Symphony of Psalms, third movement, 2 before 17 (choral parts only). Copyright 1931 by Edition Russe de Musique; renewed 1958. Copyright and renewal assigned to Boosey & Hawkes, Inc. Revised edition copyright by Boosey & Hawkes, Inc. Renewed 1975. Reprinted by permission of Boosey & Hawkes, Inc.

Lau- dá- te DÓ- MI- NUM, lau- dá- te É- um.

Example 23: Igor Stravinsky, *Concerto per due pianoforti soli*, fourth movement, subject and answer. Copyright B. Schott's Soehne, Mainz, 1936. Copyright renewed 1964. All rights reserved. Used by permission of European American Music Distributors Corporation, sole U.S. agent for B. Schott's Soehne.

§VII

One of the most characteristic of the folklore-derived techniques governing Stravinsky's Russian text settings (and his settings of other languages thereafter) involved the molding of a thematic phrase on the correct declamation of a "model" verse or stanza, which phrase then carries succeeding lines strictly according to syllabification—i.e., "number"—and without regard to stress. The technique is an adaptation from such *pribaútki*-like pattersongs as the following, a "humorous song" entitled "Vavila" from Linyova's anthology (ex. 24).

To trace this technique adequately in Stravinsky's work requires access to sketch material in quantity, something that is still beyond reach. A single deductive example from *Renard* will have to suffice for now, though I am willing to predict that the pervasiveness of the technique I am about to demonstrate will be amply confirmed when more material comes to light.

The first section of *Renard* to have been completed, as Stravinsky for once correctly recalled, was the concluding pattersong that follows the slaying of the vixen (figs. 81–90). Looking back upon this passage, Stravinsky called it a "pribaoutki" (*sic*).[46] It was not he who categorized it thus, however, but Afanasiev himself. For the text here is taken not from the animal stories in volume 1 of the *Russian Folk Tales* that furnished the rest of *Renard,* but from the same appendix in volume 5 that had previously served as source for the set actually entitled *Pribaoutki,* and also for the song "Ducks, Swans and Geese" in the *Trois histoires pour enfants,* which were composed at the same time as *Renard* and shared space with it in Stravinsky's sketchbooks.[47] Of his setting, Stravinsky said that it "exploits a speed and an accentuation that are natural to Russian," and warned that "no translation of this passage can translate what I have done musically with the language."[48] And that is true. Yet if one looks at the passage in question, one notes that, as usual, most of the stresses in the very first line have been moved out of place (ex. 25).[49] There is in fact nothing "natural to Russian" about this accentuation.

46. *Conversations with Stravinsky,* p. 35.

47. The *pribaútka* in *Renard* is found on pp. 238–39 in the 1913 edition of Afanasiev, vol. 5 (see note 43); the one in the *Trois histoires,* on p. 237. In the standard Soviet editions (eds. Azadovsky, Andreev, and Sokolov [Academia, 1936]; reedited by Vladimir Propp [Moscow, 1957]), they are nos. 542 and 537 respectively.

48. *Conversations,* p. 35.

49. Stravinsky has replaced Afanasiev's first words, *Kukolka, kukolka* (little doll) with two poetic diminutives of "vixen"—*lisynka-lisitsa*—to tie the *pribaútka* to the *Renard* theme, an impressive demonstration of his command of the language of *skazki.*

Example 24: Evgeniia Linyova, *Velikorusskie pesni v narodnoi garmonizatsii* (Saint Petersburg, 1909), vol. 2, p. 65.

[Trans.: 12. I stood by the cathedral doors, the bishop himself fell in love with me.
13. Two priests' sons went crazy, two clergymen went into their dance.
14. The priest tripped on his chasuble, the sacristan lost count of the church bells.]

Example 25: Igor Stravinsky, *Renard*. Reprinted by permission of Belwin Publishers.

Lí- syn'- ka, li- sí- tsa! Glia- chá dól- go ne zhi- lá?

In a brief description of the *Renard* sketches, Robert Craft informs us that the draft, dated 16 January 1916, carries the heading "Pribautki: Gospodi pomilui." Recognizing the latter pair of words as the Slavonic Kyrie, Craft speculated that *Renard* was to have been originally "a religious satire that was later diluted or bowdlerized."[50] But that is not the case. All the heading meant was that Stravinsky began his setting of Afanasiev's *pribaútka* not with the main text but with a variant given by Afanasiev in a footnote, which is now to be found not at the beginning of the section of *Renard,* but near the end, at fig. 87 (ex. 26). The setting of this group of lines, the first to have been composed, is irreproachable from the prosodic standpoint. It provided the model stanza, to which other lines were fitted purely syllabically, not accentually (ex. 27).

50. *Stravinsky in Pictures and Documents*, p. 139.

Example 26: Igor Stravinsky, *Renard*, rehearsal 87. Reprinted by permission of Belwin Publishers.

Gó- spo- di po- mí- lui, Na kó- ni- ke Da- ní- lo

Example 27a–e: Igor Stravinsky, *Renard,* the concluding *pribaútka*. Reprinted by permission of Belwin Publishers.

Example 27a: rehearsal 83

Lí- syn'- ka, li- sí- tsa, Po- dí po- vó- di- tsu

Example 27b: rehearsal 84

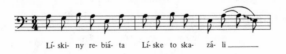

Lí- ski- ny re- biá- ta Lí- ske to ska- zá- li _____

Example 27c: 2 after 85

Mu- zhík pés- niu spel... _____ Na ka- púst- nik sel. _____

Richard Taruskin

Example 27d: rehearsal 88

V pe- chí ka- la- chí, Kak o- gón' gor- ia chí

Example 27e: rehearsal 89

Na- é- kha- li bo- iá- re da so- bák na- vez- lí

51. It was brought to my attention by my colleague,
Prof. Jack Beeson.

Without knowledge of the sketches for the Renard *pribaútka* it would not be possible to identify the *Gospodi pomilui* verse, buried as it now is in the middle of things, as the model stanza from which the other, prosodically distorted, verses were derived. (Nor is this the only time that Stravinsky, in proceeding from sketch to finished composition, covered his methodological tracks.) Yet having discovered the technique, one encounters it again and again, sometimes in very surprising contexts. Consider the rather famously awkward prosody of Anne's aria, "Quietly, night," in the third scene of *The Rake's Progress*. The beginning of the second stanza contains one of Stravinsky's most notorious "lapses" in English prosody (ex. 28).[51] The lapse involves more than accentuation. It also involves syntax. The end of the first sentence is detached from the rest and set along with the beginning of the second sentence in a single unbroken melodic arch. It seems inconceivable that this music was written to these words.

In fact, it was not. The aria is in a modified strophic form with coda. The second stanza begins with a truncated recapitulation of the music to which the first had been set. Stravinsky's sketches show how literally this was the case: the words of the second stanza were initially overlaid to the sketches of the first (ex. 29). The offending phrase of music had originally carried the text of the last line of the first stanza: "Although I weep, it knows of loneliness." And the sketch page reproduced in example 30a shows the original model stanza: except for one minor pecadillo (the accentuation of "although") it is quite blameless as to prosody—far more so, in fact, than the setting of the line as it finally took shape in the finished score— another instance of Stravinsky covering his tracks (ex. 30b). What seems especially interesting is the apparent retroactive influence of the setting of "warmly be the same" in the second stanza on that of "although I weep" in the first. (The change is entered explicitly at the very top of example 29.)

Of course, ignoring punctuation was nothing new to Stravinsky by the time he wrote *The Rake's Progress*. The Russian settings abound with examples, and so,

194

Example 28: Igor Stravinsky, *The Rake's Progress,* Anne's aria (act 1, scene 3), beginning of second stanza. Libretto by W. H. Auden and Chester Kallman. Copyright 1949, 1950, 1951 by Boosey & Hawkes, Inc.; renewed 1976, 1977, 1979. Reprinted by permission of Boosey & Hawkes, Inc.

Example 29: Igor Stravinsky, sketch for Anne's aria (Paul Griffiths et al., *The Rake's Progress* [Cambridge, 1982], plate 6). Reprinted by permission of the Paul Sacher Foundation.

of course, do Russian folk songs. But in *The Rake* (or in *Oedipus* or *Perséphone,* for that matter) it gets noticed, and Stravinsky gets criticized for it by those who tacitly, perhaps unwittingly, approach his work with the assumptions and the desiderata of a César Cui. Our assumptions, however, ought to be the opposite.

Example 30: Igor Stravinsky, *The Rake's Progress.* Libretto by W. H. Auden and Chester Kallman. Copyright 1949, 1950, 1951 by Boosey & Hawkes, Inc.; renewed 1976, 1977, 1979. Reprinted by permission of Boosey & Hawkes, Inc.

For Stravinsky, once he had made his "rejoicing discovery," the accents of spoken language were merely there to be manipulated like any other musical parameter, for the sake of musical enjoyment. "Words," he asserted in one of his more belligerent

Example 30a: "Model stanza" transcribed from top of above sketch.

Although I weep,_____ it knows of lone- li- ness

Example 30b: The same line, final version in published score.

al- though I weep,___ it ___ knows, it knows of lone- li- ness.

52. "M. Igor Stravinsky nous parle de 'Perséphone,'" *Excelsior* (Paris), 1 May 1934 (rpt. White, *Stravinsky,* p. 534).

53. One of the early musical impressions Stravinsky recorded in *Chroniques de ma vie* seems to have been rather transparently "planted" to justify this modernist predilection. Recalling the song of an ancient, near-dumb peasant singer, Stravinsky describes it as having been "composed of two syllables, the only ones he could pronounce; they were devoid of meaning, but he made them alternate with incredible dexterity" (*Chronicle of My Life* [London, 1936], p. 11). Here is one good example among many of Stravinsky's way of manufacturing "formative influences" to suit his changing aesthetic purposes.

54. The wording here follows "Pushkin: Poetry and Music" (rpt. White, p. 543); Stravinsky first quoted the retort in *Chroniques,* p. 117.

manifestos, "far from helping, constitute for the musician a burdensome intermediary. . . . For music is not thought."[52] Instead, he maintained, he sought syllables, that is, lingual sounds to match with musical sounds.[53] For if, as Mallarmé put it to Degas in a phrase that so delighted Stravinsky that he quoted it twice in his published writings, "one does not create rhymes with ideas but with words,"[54] then one does not create music with words but with sounds—or at least Stravinsky did not. In this, as in so many other ways, he sought in the aesthetic stance of folk artists the seeds and the validation of an authentic modernism. Though it may discomfit us that he saw fit to set the poetry of Auden or of Gide as if it were a Russian limerick, that is what he did, and seriously. To fail to take this aspect of his art seriously is to fail at a very basic level to understand it.

POSTSCRIPT (MAY 1983)

Through the good offices of the Special Collections staff at the Music Division of the New York Public Library, temporary custodian of the Stravinsky archive (and I wish specially to thank Richard Koprowski, John Shepard, and Susan T. Sommer), I have at last gained access to some of the sketch material relevant to the propositions advanced deductively in the foregoing essay, and I can make a few refinements and amplifications in light of it.

Stravinsky, it seems, used scansion marks to plan his prosody as early as the first act of *Le rossignol* (1908–9), so it would seem that I may have overstated the case somewhat with respect to the direct influence of Sakharov on his methods. On the other hand, the original setting of *Shchuka* was indeed conceived as I predicted. The syllables marked long by Sakharov were calculated (as per Linyova's prescription) to fall on downbeats, or at least on explicit secondary stresses within a longer measure.

The earliest sketches for the *Podbliudnye* are found in a tiny notebook (no. 14a in the catalog prepared for Stravinsky's use in 1954 by Robert Craft and later published as appendix C in Eric Walter White's *Stravinsky: The Composer and His Works*), which also contains notations for a few other works—the *Berceuses du chat*, the "Chant dissident" from *Quatre chants russes,* and the *Berceuse* to Stravinsky's daughter Liudmila. This notebook, despite its heterogeneous contents, has a delightful painted cover (such as one often finds among the manuscripts of the Swiss years) giving the title "Podbliudnye" and a little floral design on a blue field. What one, with some surprise, finds first in it are the four texts for the choruses copied out on four successive rectos in the order of the finished set, although the settings were composed in a different order, over a span of almost three years. The first to be composed (as noted already in the body of the paper, above), was *Shchuka* (no. 3), immediately followed in the sketchbook by the fourth chorus, *Puzishche* (usually translated as "Master Portly"). Here sketches for the *Podbliudnye* leave off. (A separate bifolium of uncertain date, inserted into a little sleeve pasted into the back cover of the book, contains early sketches for *Ovsen,* the second of the set. For sketches to the first chorus—*U Spasa v Chigasakh,* which Stravinsky may have remembered from Pushkin's *Eugene Onegin,* chapter 5 [the eighth stanza], and which Nabokov translates "At Our Savior's parish in Chigasy, beyond the Yauza"—one must go to a different, somewhat later sketchbook [Craft no. 16b], otherwise given over to *Renard,* the four-handed piano pieces, the "Song of the Bear" with a dedication to "Svetik," i.e., Stravinsky's son Sviatoslav [Soulima], and other works, some unrealized.)

The sketches for *Shchuka* show Stravinsky tackling the song phrase by phrase in two consecutive drafts. Both curiously stop after the fifth phrase (out of seven), and the first draft is missing the first phrase (possibly because a leaf has slipped out of the sketchbook). The leading part of the second, more complete, draft is given below (ex. 31) as far as the third phrase, for comparison with example 17 above. Sakharov's scansion marks have been added.

The most salient rhythmic difference between this sketch and the published version consists of the dactyls in the first and third phrases, which mirror Sakharov's stresses quantitatively as well as tonically. The telltale second syllable of "Novagoroda" is on the downbeat as per Linyova (one would give much, of

Example 31: Igor Stravinsky, sketch for *Shchuka*. Reproduced by permission of the Paul Sacher Foundation.

Shchú- ka shla iz No- va- gó- ro- da Sla- va! O- na khvost vo- lo-

-klá iz Be- la- Ó- ze- ra Sla- va! Kak u shchú- ki che- shúi- ka se-

-ré- bran- na- ia Sla- va!

course, to see the missing first draft of that word, assuming one existed), and the only reason why "khvost" in the second phrase is not so placed seems to be a general avoidance in this setting of measures shorter than 2/4. (The breaking up of the 5/8 bars in the 1954 revision is in keeping with many of Stravinsky's late-period rebarrings; a good example is the 1943 *Danse sacrale,* where so many "fives," of whatever beat value, are broken down into twos and threes.)

The final version of *Shchuka* arrived at in 1914 or thereafter (it is found complete among Stravinsky's manuscripts only in a fair copy of the complete set, though the first phrase alone is found on a very decorative, painted loose sheet on the other side of a sketch for *Les noces*) is identical to the one published in 1930, but for one extremely telling detail. The first phrase is given as it appears on the loose sheet (ex. 32), for comparison with example 17a above.

Example 32: Igor Stravinsky, *Shchuka*, final version. Reproduced by permission of the Paul Sacher Foundation.

Shchú- ka shla iz No- va- gó- ro- da

The 8/8 bar is there, all right, but it is broken up by the dotted bars in a way that preserves the Sakharov scansion and, moreover, clearly guided Stravinsky's 1954 revision. The dotted bars resolve the discrepancy between examples 17a and 17b, and one can only wonder why they were omitted from the 1930 edition (the more so as all the other measures longer than 6/8 in that edition do have dotted bars to guide the conductor's beat and, presumably, the choir's accentuation).

Although it is not strictly germane to our theme, it is very interesting to compare the two drafts of *Shchuka* in the 1914 sketchbook. The comparison reveals that the starkly homorhythmic texture so characteristic of the *Podbliudnye* was something attained, rather than (as it would be natural to assume) integral to the "neo-nationalist" concept. Phase 2 in the earlier sketch goest as per ex. 33.

Imitation and cross-accent are both so foreign to the nature of these songs as we know them that it is astonishing to find them a part of the original conception.

Example 33: Igor Stravinsky, sketch for *Shchuka,* second phrase. Reproduced by permission of the Paul Sacher Foundation.

How much more conventional this early thought is than the ascetically plain published version. But only by knowing the sketches can we see this plainness for the "second simplicity" it is. It is an inspiring example of Stravinsky's creative ruthlessness, reminding us of the force with which *Apollo* struck Balanchine: "It seemed to tell me that I could dare not to use everything, that I, too, could eliminate." That, if anything, is "the Message of Igor Stravinsky."

Index